IMAGES
of America

RAPID CITY

HISTORIC DOWNTOWN ARCHITECTURE

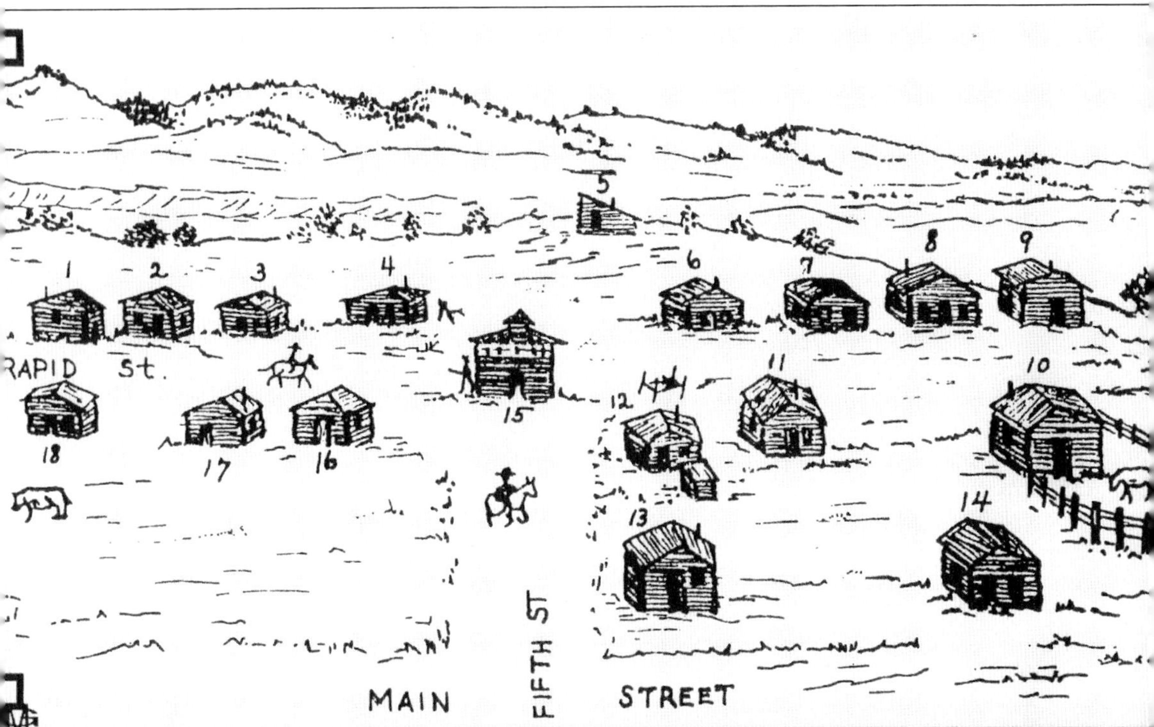

pid City as it appeared in the year of its birth 1876. Drawing was made by George B. Mansfield, cam
pid City in 1883. The Block house in the center about the intersection of 5th Street and the railroad tr
John W. Allen and Jake Clausen; 2. John Brennan & Oscar Nicholson; 3. Reddy Johnson; 4. Noah Newba
Far north leantype cabin, man named Lee; 6. Man named Bunker; 7. Frank P. Moulton, later Sheriff &
arshal; 8. Captain E. Legro; 9. Sam Scott; 10. The village stable and corral; 11. Rufus Madison; 12. A b
own as Dutch Joe; 13. John G. Smith and Will E. Smith; 14. Jacob Leddy; 15. Blockhouse; 16,17,18, to
Blockhouse in the second row from back were for visitors and transients

George Mansfield drew this map of early Rapid City.

On the cover: The Buell Building is the most identifiable and photographed structure in Rapid City because of its eclectic nature, especially the "onion dome" gracing an ornate oriel window. It combines Italianate and Romanesque Revival elements created using locally acquired and crafted materials. Located at the corner of Seventh and St. Joseph Streets, it has stood since 1888 as the iconic architectural symbol of the city. (Courtesy of the Minnilusa Historical Association.)

IMAGES
of America

RAPID CITY

HISTORIC DOWNTOWN ARCHITECTURE

Adrienne Merola Kerst,
Jean Oleson-Kessloff,
and Patrick D. Roseland

ARCADIA
PUBLISHING

ISBN 978-0-7385-4140-2

Published by Arcadia Publishing
Charleston, South Carolina

Printed in the United States of America

Library of Congress Catalog Card Number: 2006933897

For all general information contact Arcadia Publishing at:
Telephone 843-853-2070
Fax 843-853-0044
E-mail sales@arcadiapublishing.com
For customer service and orders:
Toll-Free 1-888-313-2665

Visit us on the Internet at www.arcadiapublishing.com

The authors dedicate their efforts to the founders and citizens of Rapid City, whose pioneering spirit built a community, not only with bricks and mortar, but also with hearts and souls. We dedicate this book to the stewards of our historic resources, who have persevered in the belief that historic architecture, the tangible expression of a community's development, is valuable and worthy of preservation, and should be available for the edification of generations to come. Therefore, the authors are donating their royalties from the sales of this book to the Minnilusa Historical Association. Finally, on a more personal note, we wish to dedicate this work to our parents, who instilled in us an appreciation for our heritage.

Contents

ACKNOWLEDGMENTS

A special thanks is extended to Reid Riner, director of Minnilusa Historical Association for his support and encouragement. His never-ending witticisms kept us laughing though the long days of research. In that research we had the opportunity to meet an incredible number of people who were very generous with their stories, pictures and expertise: Minnilusa Pioneer Museum; Mary Farrar, Fred W. Farrar Collection; Ben P. R. Roose; Arvada Center, City of Arvada, Colorado, Collins Collection; Bill Grothe; Sheri Sponder, editorial assistant, *Rapid City Journal*; Pastor Wilbur Holz and staff, Trinity Lutheran Church; Bruce Dahl, Montana-Dakota Utilities Company; Steve McCarthy, MAC Construction Company, Inc.; Deanne Farrar, Christian Science Church; Gene Williams, Rapid City Laundry; Mary Woelfee, Rapid City Regional Hospital; Gordon Paulson, president, Telco Pioneers, Blue Bell Council; Fred Thurston, AIA, and Dick McConnell, AIA, enVision Design; Alan K. Lathrop, Northwest Architectural Archives, University of Minnesota; Steve Colgan, NWE Management Company; Troy Erickson, M. G. Oil Company; John Morrison, Motor Service Company; Walter Bradsky; Helen Wrede; Kathy Didier, Hotel Alex Johnson; Jerry and Jolaine Tracy; Jill Pudwill, TSP, Sioux Falls; Chris Nelson, historic preservation specialist and Matthew Reitzel, manuscript archivist, South Dakota State Historical Society; Vince Baumgartner; Helen Hoyt; Pastor Jeff Otterman, St. James Lutheran Church, Belle Fourche; Kevin Eilbeck, Aurora Studios, Inc; Phil Hunter, Curt Bechtel, Brad Solon, Rise Ficken and Sharlene Mitchell, Growth Management Department, City of Rapid City; the Koppmann Family, North Western Warehouse Company; Beth Kukuk, First Presbyterian Church; Brian Bade, Storyteller West; the Roseland Collection; Kevin Randall, Rapid Chevrolet; Robert Knecht; Vina M. Niemann Collection; Eka Parkison; Randy Aker; Rapid City Elks Lodge 1187; Sandra Burke, AIA; Rhonda Buell Schier; the Behrens family; Bud Olsen; Paulette Montileaux, curator, Sioux Indian Museum; Donovin Sprague Hump, historian; Lee Geiger, AIA, Geiger Architecture, architectural advisor; Norman Nelson, copy editor and historian; and of course, our spouses, Jim Kerst and Bill Kessloff, who persevered with us. Also, too numerous to mention, are many friends and family members who provided support and encouragement. To everyone mentioned herein and anyone we may have inadvertently forgotten to mention, we owe you all our sincerest gratitude.

INTRODUCTION

These old buildings do not belong to us only, that they have belonged to our forefathers, and they will belong to our descendants unless we play them false. They are not in any sense our property to do as we like with. We are only trustees for those that come after us.

—William Morris

The built environment is an important, tangible reminder of our history. It is an indicator of change through time, of aesthetics, of popular and not-so-popular styles, and of the economics of boom and bust. Architecture reveals the psychology of a community, its values and social structure, all of which are important aspects in growing a city. Architecture impacts education, culture, society, politics, the environment and, obviously, history.

Rapid City's downtown buildings reflect countless dreams of frontier people given substance by architects and builders and imbued with soul by residents and occupants. If walls could talk the buildings of this city would recount with pride an impressive history.

The historic downtown core of Rapid City is listed on the National Register of Historic Places. The national register is the nation's official list of cultural resources worthy of recognition and preservation. Rapid City's downtown is comprised of a wonderfully intact stock of historic buildings that incorporate a multitude of architectural styles exemplifying the continual dedication of its residents to make this once-frontier town a permanent and monumental expression of their pioneering spirit and cowboy ingenuity.

Rapid City's geographical location provided availability and abundance of natural resources, a viable water supply and proximity to major trade routes. The city's original six-block town site was laid out in late February 1876 along Rapid Creek by a group of savvy entrepreneurs drawn here with the vision of a "new Denver." Three of these founders—Samuel Scott, John Brennan, and Thomas Ferguson—remained in the fledgling community, attaining positions of notability and helping grow the town in its earliest days.

Laid out in a grid, East Boulevard marked the easternmost limit of the original city and so it was in each of the other directions, North and South Streets and West Boulevard. The core of downtown began on Main Street between Sixth and Seventh Streets, the location of the original town site. Rapid City's downtown became multi-functional, having the availability of goods and services to address all the needs of a community in one location. This is reflected in the two types of buildings found: storefront and institutional. Storefront businesses include retail, wholesale, food service and accommodations, whereas institutional structures include government offices, schools, hospitals, and the like.

Initially business people took on design responsibilities working in tandem with local tradesmen to build both public and private buildings. Frontier buildings were simple log and wood structures, many with false fronts, built quickly to meet the basic need for shelter. This is reflected in the 1876 Mansfield map showing log buildings surrounding a protective blockhouse. As the city grew, so did the pool of professional architects, drafts persons, and specialty crafts persons who lived and worked locally. Buildings then took on a more sophisticated and urban appearance. Three Rapid City architects whose works are still widely distributed around the city were H. E. Waldron, James Ewing, and Adrian Forrette. Other professionals were commissioned who had no connection to Rapid City, but were notables in their field, including: Harold Spitznagel of Sioux Falls, whose outstanding project in Rapid City was Trinity Lutheran Church; Edward Oldefest from Chicago, commissioned by Alex Johnson to build his grand hotel; J. P. Eisentraut, designer of the Elks building was from Iowa, but practiced in South Dakota for almost 20 years; John Wheeler of St. Paul, Minnesota, worked extensively for the Catholic church; Harry Edbrooke of Denver, a Christian Scientist, was commissioned to design the Christian Science church here; F. V. Thomas designed the Fairmont Creamery; the T. E. Ibberson Company's architects specialized in agricultural processing facilities such as Tri-State Milling and Aby's; W. E. Hulse, who practiced widely in Iowa and Nebraska, designed the 1922 Pennington County Courthouse; Federal government architects James Knox Taylor and Waldo Winter came to Rapid City to build the Federal building and the Works Progress Administration Sioux Indian Museum, respectively.

Architectural progression from frontier town to regional urban focus and thriving tourist destination occurred in various periods of development, three of which are reflected in distinct architectural styles within the commercial district. The first period, from 1884 to 1920 is divided into two phases, with the first, the 1880s through the 1890s, exhibiting the Victorian influences of Italianate, Romanesque, and Queen Anne styles, and the latter phase, 1900 to 1920, showing the emergence of the Chicago school, craftsman, Beaux-Arts, classical revival, and utilitarian influences.

The second period occurred from 1920 through the early 1940s and contains examples of art deco, utilitarian, moderne, and international stylistic trends. The last period, 1950 into the 1980s and beyond, exhibits primarily modern, contemporary styles as well as updated facades applied to the fronts of older structures.

Surviving structures are predominately utilitarian in nature. Still, the general character is late 19th century, as determined by the majority of landmark buildings being Victorian or vernacular expressions of Victorian-era high styles. They display the significant, character-defining features indicative of that general historic period, including decorative elaborations, rich detailing, and verticality of design. These buildings are usually found on corners of important intersections. It was in the use of local materials in the hands of local designers and craftsman that the distinctive and unique character of these structures and therefore the city came to fruition.

Lumber from the hills was transported to the many lumber mills in Rapid City. The best known of these were Warren Lamb, Lampert, Lanphere, Fish and Hunter, Robbins and Sterns, Daniel's, and Knecht's, all of whom supplied the growing community with other basic building materials in addition to lumber.

As wood construction gave way to masonry, especially during the 1880s building boom, many quarries and brickyards came into existence near the town. All drew on the geological wealth deposited in the Black Hills. Evans Sandstone Quarry in Hot Springs produced fine sandstone, as did other sandstone quarries in Fall River County. However, sandstone was also quarried in Rapid City about two miles northwest of town at Burton's and at a location described to be two-to-three miles below the city. Numerous brickyards were in operation at any given time and sometimes could barely keep up with demand. In Rapid City, the best known were Marshall's, Louis Volin's, and Armstrong and Dent's. Quarnberg's of Belle Fourche also made quality bricks utilized on many buildings here.

In historical accounts, mention is made of deposits of beautifully colored marble in the vicinity of Deadwood; with the same being found six-to-eight miles outside of Rapid City.

Abundance of limestone led to the establishment of a state-owned cement plant near the city. This was especially important when the use of quarried rock, such as granite, became too costly. Concrete block and molded concrete formed and decorated buildings and paved early streets.

A building boom coincided with the arrival of the railroad as commonly occurs. But as technologies progressed and the automobile became the dominant form of transportation, the Black Hills and Rapid City became sought-after destinations. The arrival of tourists heralded a building boom of another sort. With an emphasis on visitor services, tourism brought its own, unique architectural forms. This developmental force is still a major factor in the success and growth of the city. Rapid City can look to its architectural heritage to help sustain its economic future. The thriving downtown and neighboring residential historic districts are increasingly important attractions to the expanding cultural heritage tourism industry. Thus, appreciating and preserving our historic architecture can no longer be perceived as an elitist pastime. It is an important contributor to our economic, as well as psychological, well-being.

It is 1886. Pictured is the Fremont, Elkhorn and Missouri Valley station, Rapid City's first railroad depot. Based on standardized plans for serving passengers and freight, the little wooden depot was built with gabled ends and bracketed open eaves. The horse-drawn trolley waits to take passengers downtown. There is plenty to see and do in the growing community. Welcome.

One

Buggies to Buses

It is a national policy to preserve for public use historic sites, buildings and objects of national (and regional) significance for the inspiration and benefit of the people.

—Historic Sites Act of 1935, United States Congress

All forms of transportation bring with them specialized buildings and structures. Architecture relative to each form of conveyance has had a presence in historic downtown Rapid City. Liveries that stabled beasts of burden along with the preferred conveyance were no more than large barns with stalls and an office in which to conduct business.

Railroads, in many cases, determined homesteading and town site locations. The first rail line reached Rapid City from the south in 1886. A railroad boom occurred between 1905 and 1907 with the arrival of eastern lines and a short line from Rapid City west to Mystic. All these railroads brought with them the construction of the facilities necessary for rail service to thrive and survive, such as passenger and freight depots. A warehouse district quickly grew up trackside for the shipping and receiving of products via rail and later by truck. Sometimes built by the railroad, they were operated by local businessmen.

With the advent of the automobile age came new forms of related architecture. Car dealerships required showrooms featuring expansive plate-glass display windows. Tire and automobile accessory businesses came into existence. Public and private garages evolved from liveries and carriage houses, providing storage and maintenance space.

As the demand for fuel increased, gas stations soon dotted almost every corner. Whether unique or of standardized design, these buildings were normally fitted with canopies extending off a relatively small building to accommodate customers who drove up under them to utilize gas pumps. A wide array of architectural styles and construction materials was utilized.

Long distance and local bus service provided another form of mass transit requiring housing. Bus stations were similar in design to rail terminals in that they provided ticketing, waiting, boarding, and luggage areas.

The Chicago and North Western Railroad, known as the "North Western," purchased the Fremont, Elkhorn and Missouri Valley Railroad in 1903. Because the depot (above) was located so far from downtown, it was determined to be an inconvenience, accessible by a horse-drawn trolley or on foot, horseback, or buggy. Thus, the former Elkhorn depot was loaded onto a rail flatbed and moved to Eighth and Rapid Streets. The wooden structure continued in use until a new brick depot was constructed. This masonry depot (below), a more substantial building, had a hip roof with deep over-hanging eaves supported by decorative brackets. The structure exhibited elements of decorative brick detailing. It was the North Western Railroad that, in the late 1920s, brought three men to Rapid City who would forever leave a mark on its history: Alex Johnson, Calvin Coolidge, and Gutzon Borglum.

This 1906 one-story, hipped-roof frame depot served the Missouri River and Northwestern Railroad, also known as the Crouch Line and Rapid Canyon Line. The building was typical of small-town, combination depots, composed of a center office flanked by passenger and freight rooms. A large bay window provided the station agent a vantage point for viewing both the platform and the tracks. Bracketed, open eaves provided some platform shelter for passengers.

At the corners of Sixth and Seventh Streets at Omaha Street, the Chicago, Milwaukee and St. Paul Railroad built its passenger and freight depots. The *c.* 1915 passenger station was like many others; it was selected from an assortment of standardized plans. Size, scale, and building materials were determined by the importance of the community as a stop on the line. This rectangular frame depot had a hip and cross gable roofline.

Black Hills Wholesale Grocery, built in 1891, is a three-story, brick Italianate located in the warehouse district. Once utilized as Crouch Line Railroad headquarters and warehouse space, it features a heavy brick cornice, pediment, and upper-story arched windows. A decorative cast iron storefront encloses large solid-pane windows with transoms. There is a projecting lintel and loading dock. Structurally, 12-inch square timber posts support 3-by-14 inch floor joists with 3-foot thick basement walls.

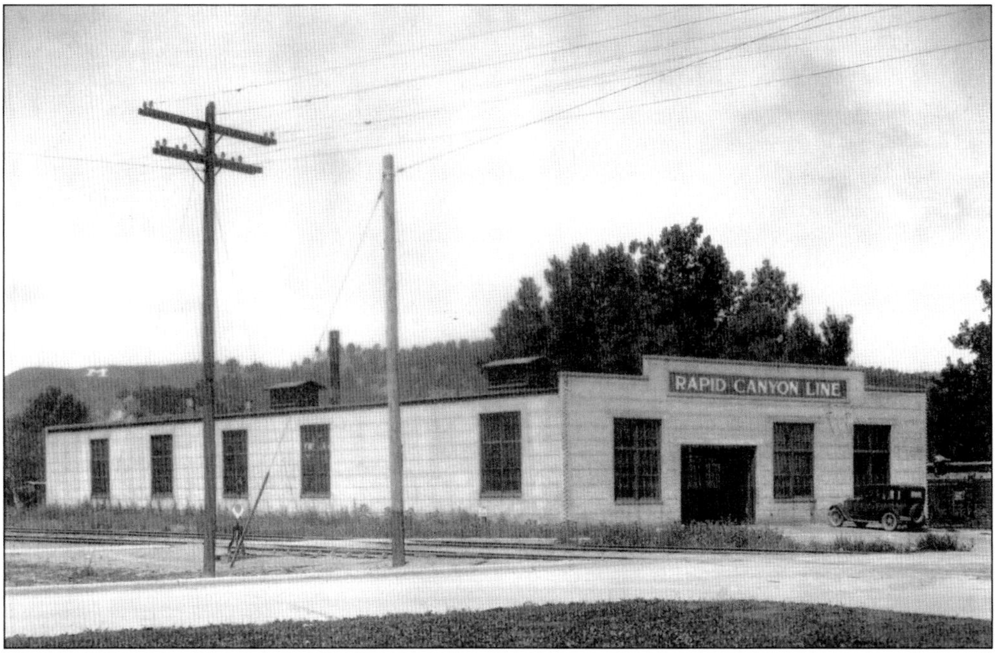

The Rapid Canyon Line built this warehouse alongside the railroad tracks near Rapid Street and West Boulevard. Constructed of brick on a rectangular plan, the main facade contained three large industrial-style windows and an oversized entry bay to accommodate vehicles. A stepped parapet conceals a flat roof with two roof monitors for additional ventilation.

This 1910 Gambrill Building represents a modest example of commercial Renaissance Revival architecture. Construction is sturdy, owing to its function as a storage warehouse, with 24-inch thick solid stone basement walls and floors capable of bearing massive loads. The south-facing main facade is symmetrical. Materials are tan brick with contrasting brown brick for details such as the segmented arched lintels around rectangular double-hung wood windows, dentils, and other decorative effects.

The 1920 Rapid City Fruit Company building, located in the original warehouse district, is comparable to surrounding structures. It is rectangular and constructed of blond cement brick with post and beam supports. Brick header courses, cornices, and corbelling, of contrasting color, are visible on two sides. Twenty-one small windows, three loading bays, four entrance doors, and a loading dock appear on various facades. A rooftop cupola houses elevator draw works.

The 1923 Chicago, Milwaukee and St. Paul Railroad brick and concrete freight house is 225 feet by 50 feet. Floor level is four feet above grade on a partial basement. The north and south elevations contain 18 and 20 freight doors, respectively, with a band of wooden multi-light windows above. The main entrance on the west facade exhibits concrete insets and coping. The low parapet conceals a long-span, bow-truss arched roof.

The Chicago and North Western Railroad constructed the 84,000 square foot, North Western Warehouse in 1932 as the first bonded public warehouse in the region. Built of brick and concrete, it is utilitarian in style with art deco influences. Four open shipping and receiving bays separated by brick pilasters mark the main facade. Six paired windows appear in the upper level. A loading platform fronts the railroad tracks.

The Adams Brothers Company, a wholesale grocery firm, was appropriately situated in the warehouse district at Eighth and Rapid Streets, adjacent to the railroad tracks. This masonry, utilitarian building housed office and warehousing space. A simple concrete-capped parapet probably hid a flat roof and possibly the housing for draw works of a freight elevator. Adams Brothers was a division of Paxton and Gallagher, who organized in 1882 in Omaha, Nebraska.

Built in 1926, Western Wholesale Liquor Company is a utilitarian-commercial-masonry-style structure. As a warehouse for distribution it incorporates a loading platform in its design. It is devoid of detail or decoration other than the concrete coping on the roofline. Its primary facade contains a central entry flanked by two large, two-light windows with awnings. A partial basement is evident. It is located at 401 Seventh Street.

Liveries were barn-like buildings that were important transportation structures prior to the automobile. They housed and cared for the horses, buggies, and wagons of travelers. The Belknap Livery was just one of many very similar structures. This frame building shows some character in the stepped parapet, hiding what appears to be a simple gable end. Two large bays accommodated conveyances and animals. The pedestrian entrance probably entered an office area.

This substantial and symmetrical Italianate building was the Bangs Livery. It was built in 1908 of sandstone block and rubble stone masonry. An elaborate bracketed cornice, with finials, supported a large inscribed pediment. Segmental arches appeared over all except the central second-story window, which displayed a Roman arch with keystone. A mid-belt plinth served as the sills for the upper-level windows. Tall, double doors accommodated animals and larger vehicles.

This highly ornate Italianate edifice housed an automobile transportation company as well as physician and real estate offices. Brick pilasters serve to separate enormous masonry storefronts and to frame a central entryway that directed clients to the businesses upstairs. A highly decorative bracketed masonry cornice supports the elaborately pedimented parapet roofline and finials. A brick dentil band runs below the cornice and above the elliptical arched upstairs windows.

The Rapid City Garage, built in 1911, was the first fireproof garage structure in town, providing service and storage for one of the first automobile dealerships and the public. Constructed of rubble stone masonry with a brick veneer, this L-shaped, three-story structure is 30 feet high, 135 feet long, and 100 feet wide. Large entry doors, reinforced floors, and a ramp to basement storage were some of its functional elements.

The Dean Motor Company building (above), constructed in 1930, is a one-and-a-half story brick and concrete structure that served as a showroom for the Dean Chevrolet Company. It is located on the southeast corner of Fourth and Main Streets. The style is described in the National Register of Historic Places as a modern, broad-front commercial type, characterized by plain concrete and brick ornamentation. The primary facade features six bays accommodating large display windows and pedestrian entrances. Arched steel trusses support a tar roof. The interior (below) is composed of two main spaces, the showroom and sales office in the front and the garage and maintenance areas in the rear. The Dean Motor Company was sold in 1931 and became McDonald Chevrolet. The name was changed around 1940 to Rapid Chevrolet Company. The business remained in this same building until 1976.

The 1929 Motor Service Company was similar to other facilities that evolved with automobile proliferation. James Ewing designed this excellent example of a brick utilitarian commercial style with art deco influences. The arched main elevation consists of three bays: two house large fixed pane display windows with transoms; the third, a central projecting arched entryway. Side elevations exhibit eight pilastered bays containing a large window, pedestrian entrance, or garage door.

These early Thunderbirds were displayed in front of Frontier Ford on Main Street in the 1950s. The Ford sales and service business was housed in this one-story, streamline-moderne building. Sharply contrasting darker-color trim panels set off the white porcelain enamel panels that give the building its crisp, clean, appealing look. Display windows, a pedestrian entryway, and a service bay make up the main facade of the business.

This site served initially as a large fuel depot for Standard Oil. Following development of gravity-fed pumps, a service station was placed here. By 1914, the company had standardized station designs. This style, the "house-with-canopy," was less objectionable when built near residential areas. This plan typically consisted of office, storage, and restrooms. Canopies provided shelter from weather. This brick and concrete station had a hip roof extending as the canopy.

Bradsky's Boulevard Super Station sat at the corner of Main Street and West Boulevard in 1935. This art deco building was constructed of brick and concrete. Both materials also provided extensive decorative detailing. The use of black-pigmented structural glass and multi-light casement windows are also indicative of art deco influence. The building incorporates service bays and a café, as well as gas islands. An outstanding feature is a rooftop domed cupola.

This *c.* 1919 advertisement for products and accessories of the automobile industry interestingly depicts the early nature of automobile-related businesses that sprang up in response to new demands: parts being sold and services being provided from a small frame shop with a large false front, attached to the owner's home.

Despite the modest venue, Rapid City's bus terminal was a Union Depot. It had two lines operating from the one building: the American and the Burlington bus lines. The structure exhibited no real style. The hipped roof portion housed passenger services, while the long span arched roof perhaps accommodated a garage and maintenance bay, and freight storage. Exterior walls are smooth stucco presumably over concrete block. Overhanging eaves provided minimal coverage for boarding and disembarking.

This is a picture of Kansas City and Eighth Streets in the 1880s.

Two

Creating Commerce

We shape our buildings; thereafter, our buildings shape us.

—Winston Churchill

Rapid City fulfilled the founder's expectations that this location would lend itself to becoming a center of travel, trade, and business. The community's historical importance as a center of commerce is apparent in its numerous fine commercial buildings.

The commercial structures of downtown Rapid City are almost all variations on the traditional American commercial storefront: that is, retail-related activities dominating the ground level, with offices and service businesses or residences located upstairs. First floor design features include storefront windows, usually of the large display type with transoms above them, recessed entries, and awnings or canopies. The typical commercial storefront is composed of several components, such as the kick plate or bulkhead, display window, transom, mid-belt cornice or molding, upper story windows, cornice, pediment, and parapet. Components vary depending on the style of the building and the materials used in its construction. Roofs, though typically flat, can be arched, hipped, or gabled. Materials vary greatly depending on the financial situation of the owner and location. Local materials were normally used but some specialty items were imported.

Styles can be indicative of the period in which a building was constructed. However, due to varying extents of local craftsmen's skills, individual interpretations, and liberties taken in the design and construction process, it is oftentimes difficult to identify a particular style, therefore vernacular expressions of high styles or eclectic forms evolve, providing local flavor. Access to numerous types of stone and timber available close at hand in the hills also contributed to the unique character of buildings in this area.

Commercial buildings were normally not taller than two or three stories, and fronts were aligned and were separated from the streets by wide sidewalks. Buildings were spaced closely together, with their walls touching or sharing common walls. Buildings were balanced with each other horizontally and vertically, some even repeating fenestration patterns, cornice lines, and other elements. That balance was disrupted when inappropriate facades were later applied in the name of modernization.

Out of this two-story, frame, false-front structure, Charles Fallon operated a paint and wallpaper shop that obviously supplied other building and decorating materials. This simple Italianate was built on a rectangular plan with the storefront at sidewalk level and living quarters upstairs. The plain cornice is overhung by a bracketed eave. An awning that spans the entire lower level conceals display windows on either side of a central doorway.

Very early commercial buildings were simple rectangular or square wooden structures that used false fronts to add a sense of grandeur to the business. The Montana Dry Goods store is one such structure. Simple Italianate details such as decorative bracketed cornices provided some individuality and unique character desired by the owner in an attempt to economically emulate the high styles of the period.

In 1886, the three-story, decorative brick Flormann Block was built at St. Joseph and Sixth Streets. This high-style Italianate structure reflected the community's growing prosperity. Large cast-iron storefronts dominated the street level. The upper stories, separated from storefronts by an ornate mid-belt cornice, consisted of 13 bays containing tall, arched windows with arched hoods. The elaborate cornice was surmounted with equally ornate pediments, finials, and roof cresting.

The corner of Eighth and St. Joseph Streets was the location of Getchell's Staple and Fancy Groceries. This two-story, wood-frame Italianate commercial structure from about 1890 is an example of early residential accommodations being located above businesses. This rectangular building exhibits classic decorative cornices with paired brackets and overhanging eaves. The storefront houses a double-door entryway with transoms framed by large, four-light, fixed-pane display windows. Note the typical locations for advertising.

In 1884, entrepreneur Robert Flormann built the Windsor Block (above) at St. Joseph and Seventh Streets. Designed in the Italianate commercial style, it is built with brick from Marshall's Brickyard, which was located outside the city limits at that time. On the primary elevation at street level, the structure consists of four bays containing four massive cast-iron storefronts with recessed entrances; each bay is divided by masonry pilasters that also support the upper level. The second story contains a set of four tall, narrow, segmentally-arched, hooded windows within each of four bays. There is a dentil course below a decorative bracketed cornice. The parapet supports pediments and finials. The central pediments identify the block, named for Flormann's business partner. A close-up of the storefront (below) reveals basement windows below display windows and a door with a staircase leading to upstairs residences or offices.

These three Italianate-style brick buildings, appropriately known as "the Italianate Trio," were constructed during a building boom between 1884 and 1888. All exhibit the heavy, decorative cornices and the tall, narrow, arched windows with elaborate window hoods definitive of this Victorian era style. The distinctive windows create an interesting lively fenestration. Storefronts were originally wooden. The buildings are located on the north side of St. Joseph Street in the 600-block.

Vann's Palace of Sweets, pictured here in 1887, once located on Main Street, was a charming, two-story brick and wood Italianate. The storefront consisted of four bays divided by brick pilasters. Display windows flanked a central entryway. The second story consisted of three bays delineated by decorative wooden columns, each containing an elliptical-arched window. A denticulate cornice and decorated parapet supported a central pediment. Reportedly, Vann's Palace of Sweets owned the only peanut roaster in town.

The Golden Rule Store, as the Web Hill Grocery and its predecessor, Siedenburg's, was known, was a small, frame, one-story commercial shop with a false front providing it with a more substantial appearance. An awning covered the entire storefront that consisted of a double-door, central entry with transom, flanked by paired, two-over-two, double-hung windows. The store was located in the 500-block on the north side of St. Joseph Street.

This frame building housed Schnasse and Gramberg's wholesale firm located on Main Street. When G. G. Schnasse was appointed postmaster in 1886, the city's post office found its second home here. The semi-circular or arched cornice, supported by paired, decorative brackets, indicates a vernacular expression of Italianate styling. The arched windows have understated window hoods, mimicking the cornice line above. A decorative porch appeared, it changed, and eventually disappeared over time.

The 1886 Clower building (above), also known as the Morris Block, is an ornate, Italianate commercial building. Once home to Big Jack Clower's Saloon, one of the most notorious drinking establishments in town, the building represents the finest extant example of high-style Italianate in the city. The intricate upper cornice, a combination of tin and wood, was likely mail ordered. The sheet metal cupola and other decorative features, such as finials and the lower level cornice, were likely ordered and finished on-site. Cast iron columns framing the large glass storefronts and supporting the second story were also probably catalog items. The upper level makes extensive use of contrasting color brick and brick patterning to attain its ornate design. Highly developed window hoods, as seen in the detail below, also contribute to the elaborate nature of the building.

One of the most prominent buildings and businesses (above) was Tom Sweeney Hardware. Built in 1886, it stood for 111 years until it was destroyed by fire in 1997. The three-story, 45,000-square-foot brick commercial Italianate housed retail and office spaces. Street level facades consisted of large, cast-iron storefronts with a corner entrance facing the intersection of Seventh and Main Streets. Windows on the upper levels were hooded with decorative segmental arches. The ornate bracketed cornice rose above a dentil row. Finials punctuated the parapet that concealed a flat roof. Tom Sweeney, pictured below on the left inside his store, was a colorful character, astute businessman, community promoter, and also a consummate marketer who utilized countless signs painted on his building for advertising purposes.

Constructed by local craftsman from a wooden mold covered with sheet copper is the Russo-Byzantine dome (right) that dominates the corner of the Buell Building at Seventh and St. Joseph Streets. Beneath the onion dome, as it is commonly referred to, is a corner oriel window. Built in 1888, the two-story eclectic Victorian-era brick structure (below) presents ornate rackets with a substantial wood and sheet metal cornice, topped with decorative pediments and finials, all indicative of Italianate styling. Brick dentils appear below the parapet roofline. Both levels contain Romanesque-style sandstone arched bays with segmental arches on the upper level. Walls are constructed of brick from Marshall's Brickyard. Three additional sections were added along Seventh Street by 1925. For a time, the building was home to the local weather station where signal flags of different colors were flown, indicating forecasted weather conditions.

This highly embellished, commercial structure was Congdon and Henry Hardware store. Built about 1890, this two-story Italianate exhibited East Lake details, also called gingerbread or spindle work, especially in extravagant window hoods and an ornate cornice. Lions' heads and finials marked an elaborate pediment over the central bay of the second story. A glass and cast-iron storefront contained a recessed entry. Stone pilasters on the main facade exhibit additional detailed carvings.

This sandstone building, once located at 621 Sixth Street, presented an imposing facade composed of a tall, cast iron-framed glass storefront with a recessed double-door entry. The second story housed symmetrically placed tall, narrow windows each with a segmental arched eyebrow. The heavy nature of the sandstone block wall was contrasted by the decorative, pressed metal cornice and pediment embossed with delicate designs.

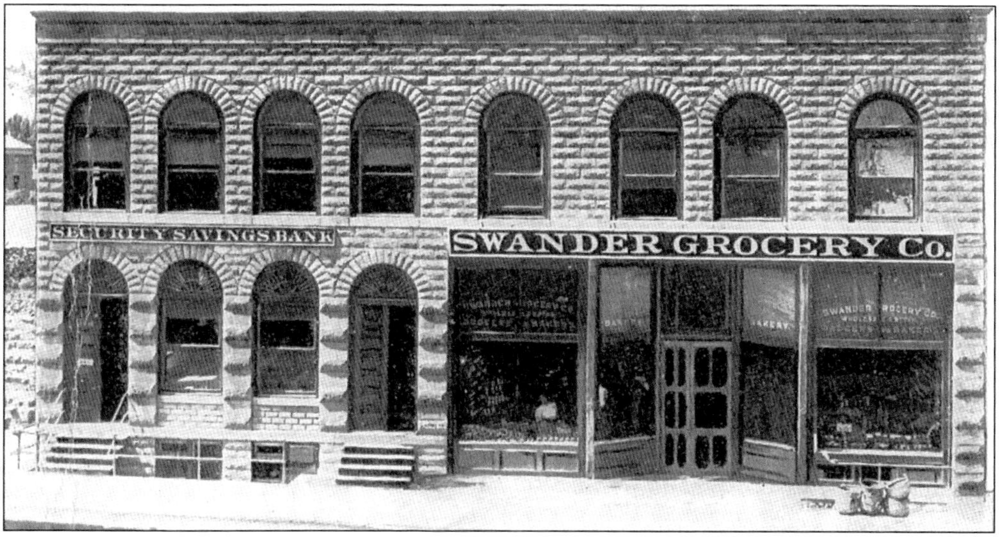

In 1905, the two-story Swander Grocery and Bakery building (above) at 517 Seventh Street was constructed in the Romanesque Revival style with the use of heavy Roman-arched surrounds over the majority of the openings. The material on the east and south elevations is simulated cut stone, made of two-foot cast concrete blocks. The remainder of the building is brick. The street level portion is a wood-framed glass storefront with cast-iron supporting columns. Opened as Swander and Jones on Main Street, the partners separated in the early 1900s and Harry Swander moved the business to this location. In 1928, the bakery relocated to St. Joseph and Twelfth Streets. The interior (below) was typical of the era; sales counters separated the customers from merchandise. Spaces were narrow and deep with high ceilings. This ceiling was pressed metal tile.

In this photograph, the COD grocery store was located on the Seventh Street side of the Buell Building. This facade of the Buell Building is a highly ornate Victorian-era Italianate with a heavy decorative cornice and parapet supporting finials and an arched pediment. Upper level windows contain stained and prismatic glass in the spaces below the decorative window hoods. A typical large storefront appears at the street level.

The high point for utilizing stained glass was between the 1870s and 1930s when a nationwide building boom created demand for stained and leaded glass windows, door panels, and transoms. Mass-produced by 1900 and available to almost everyone, mail order specialty catalogs assured shoppers that their glass was made-to-order. This Buell Building transom advertises the business name in stained glass.

Rapid City Implement Company (above) opened in 1907 at the northwest corner of Main and Eighth Streets in a two-story, typical Italianate commercial structure. The lower level on the main facade contained display windows and two recessed entrances. The windows on the second level exhibited pedimented hoods. A parapet roofline with finials and an elaborate, dated pediment rose above the wide, decorative cornice. An interesting feature was the pressed metal siding sheathing the entire structure. A brick pattern was imitated in the metal as seen below. This cladding became popular in the early 20th century. Purchased in lumberyards or ordered from a supplier's catalog, it was reasonably priced, easy to install, came in various patterns, and required little maintenance, although painting was required to prevent rusting and repair of damaged sheets was difficult.

In 1915, the Farlow Block burned in the fire that also destroyed the neighboring Pennington County Bank. Like the bank, it was eclectic, combining stylistic elements of Italianate and Romanesque in sandstone and brick. The street level accommodated three storefronts, while offices occupied the upstairs. Leaded glass appeared within the arches above eight second-story windows. Following the fire, the new Haines Block was built around the new Pennington County Bank.

The Haines Block on Sixth Street, designed by H. E. Waldron, was built in 1918. The style is utilitarian with art deco ornamentation. This three-story brick and stone building contains four storefronts. Six-over-one double-hung windows appear on the second and third floors. The decorative molding and coping is concrete. The L-shaped building wraps around the neoclassical revival Pennington County Bank, presenting a second facade on Main Street.

This *c.* 1907 view (above) of the south side of Main Street shows a row of structures with elaborately decorated pediments. Appearing on the roof edge and usually triangular, as in the building on the above left, pediments can take any shape. These pediments are decorated with scrolls, rosettes, and finials exhibiting Italianate influence. The decorative cornice, carved brackets, and molding, as seen below, add to the effect, making for an impressive view.

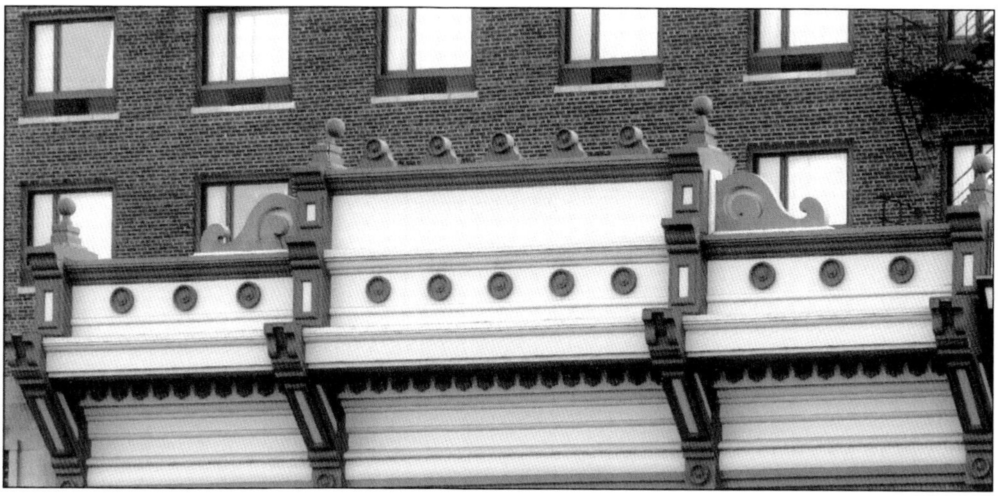

Pete Sweeney's Bar was once located on Main Street. Architecturally eclectic, it combined the Romanesque Revival style with Italianate decorative features as noted in the cornice and bracketed overhanging eave. Constructed of rubble stone masonry with a sandstone facade, this two-story building had a cast-iron storefront with prismatic glass transoms. Above that, a cast-iron lintel supported the upper story where two paired windows with heavy Romanesque arches appeared.

This highly ornate false-front with finials sits atop the simple, single-story wood building that housed Foster's Barber Shop. Braced from the rear, the false-front, made of pressed metal, concealed a front gable structure. Almost always used for commercial purposes, false-fronts were vertical extensions of a building beyond its roofline intended to make it look more impressive. The additional height also added visual continuity of scale and rhythm along the streetscape.

McNamara Brothers' Bookstore was located at 615 Main Street. Built in 1919, replacing their wooden building, this brick commercial vernacular structure presents neoclassical influences evident in the parapet roofline and the second story bays, which house two windows between pilastered columns in antis. At street level, the storefront facade is composed of two portions, the display windows flanking a recessed central entryway and the tall, prismatic glass transoms above.

The use of prismatic glass transoms was popular from the 1890s through the 1930s. They served as a decorative means of directing light into buildings' interiors. Ridged patterns on the inside surfaces of a glass tile refracted entering sunlight towards the back of interior spaces. Tiles were joined with lead or zinc cames as used in stained glass windows. Prismatic glass became obsolete with expanded use of electric lighting.

The Web Hill Company (above) was one of several businesses that occupied this Main Street location and sold all manner of dry goods. This 1925 photograph shows a two-story, brick and sandstone utilitarian commercial building with a 50-foot storefront at the street level. Three display windows separate two recessed entryways. A third outside entry lead upstairs to a doctor's office. The upper floor contains four tripartite windows. Above the nameplate, prismatic glass transoms are decorative as well as practical for infusing light well into the interior space. That space is 140 feet deep, with high, pressed metal ceilings and moldings. Cast-iron columns run the length of the building. The company's business office as well as inventory storage occupied a mezzanine level, as seen in the picture below. Designed by H. E. Waldron in 1915, it later housed the J. C. Penney Company for many years.

The rock garden grotto craze that swept the Midwest from 1910 to 1930 made for interesting fountain architecture (above) at Doherty Drug. By the early 1920s, almost every drug store had a full service soda fountain and would have likely offered meals. This brick, utilitarian-style building (below) has the typical drug store entrance, the type you might see in almost any town across the United States. A prismatic glass transom announcing Drugs, and a horizontal neon sign indicating Drugs along with an arrow over the entry, ensured that a passerby would not mistake their establishment for anything other than a drugstore.

Housing the furniture and undertaking businesses of Henry Behrens, this building was a frame, vernacular expression of the Italianate style. Located at 618 Main Street, it had a recessed, double-door entry, flanked by two nine-light display windows. Decorative brackets supported mid-belt and roofline cornices. Second-story double doors are flanked by two tall four-over-four double-hung windows. Behrens came from Wisconsin in 1879 to establish one of Rapid City's earliest family businesses.

The visually unique decorative cornice and parapet roofline immediately draw viewers' attention to this masonry vernacular commercial building at 618 Main Street. Built in two phases, the eastern two-thirds, built in 1925, are alike. Tripartite windows on the upper level differentiate the western one-third, built in 1928. Although utilitarian in style, it is reminiscent of Italianate design. Three wooden storefronts have housed numerous businesses over the years, including Behrens Mortuary.

A distributor of heavy equipment, machinery, and other construction-related items, Western Material Company was located just east of downtown in 1928. Typical of light industrial businesses, the building accommodated its function: built large and spacious, to serve the display, sales style, and storage needs for such inventory. Wood construction on a rectangular or square plan with little in the way of decoration or detail marked the building type.

This utilitarian-style brick building has had many uses over the years. What started out as an automobile service building ended up as a music store prior to its demolition in the 1980s. It had a single door entrance, flanked by large double windows with transoms and what looks to be bays on each end. Decorative brickwork and an arched parapet give this building an art deco appearance.

The Kash Shoe Store was located at 624 St. Joseph Street in a small brick and wood building that was a vernacular expression of the Italianate style. The cornice was plain wood with decorative wood brackets. A fabric awning spanned the traditional storefront that had a recessed entry and large pane display windows. Signage and advertising dominated the building. This photograph probably dates from the early 1900s.

The finest example of Chicago style architecture in Rapid City is the 1909 Duhamel Building, at St. Joseph and Sixth Streets. Built by noteworthy local entrepreneur Peter Duhamel, it expressed the trend toward modernism by using reinforced steel framing. The load bearing capacity allows for expansive window surfaces, stability for large flat roofs, and immense open spaces desirable in commercial buildings. Second-story tripartite windows are indicative of the Chicago style.

The Hall building at 609 St. Joseph Street is a 1920s to 1930s art deco stone veneer over an earlier building, most likely an Italianate, built in 1884. The upper levels of this four-story structure exhibit four recessed bays containing three-over-one, double hung windows located between five fluted pilasters topped by decorative geometric patterns, relief carvings, and dentils. A stone block parapet rises above a flat roof.

The building at 613 Main Street was originally a two-story Italianate. The art deco facade, exhibiting strong verticality, is a stone veneer added at some point in the 1920s or 1930s. On the now three-story building, the upper two stories exhibit the deco designs. Geometric patterns and decorative floral relief panels appear at the top of the structure. Four recessed bays contain four-over-one, double-hung windows. Art deco architecture exhibits dynamic geometry, ornament, texture, and symbolism.

Rapid City Laundry, a fine example of streamlined art deco styling, exhibits simple ornamentation, pilasters accentuating the vertical aspects of the structure and a stepped, parapet roofline. The 1929 single-story building, designed by local architect James Ewing, is stucco over concrete block and brick. The main facade is symmetrical, exhibiting a modern, broad front. The central, projecting entry bay is flanked by two recessed bays, each containing two six-over-six windows.

The *Black Hills Daily Journal*, the newspaper that eventually became the *Rapid City Journal*, was first published in 1878 from a log cabin. At its present location of 507 Main Street, the newspaper's office building has seen various stylistic incarnations including this playful Tudor veneer applied over a rectangular brick utilitarian structure. A second story was added in 1931. The building has expanded several times since then.

The corner entrance to Gambles, built in the mid-1940s, makes this structure different from most commercial buildings. This utilitarian style brick building has a moderne-influenced recessed entrance. Large glass block transoms with casement windows top three entrance doors flanked by plate glass windows with headers of metal ribbing that is repeated in the large metal canopy that steps down at the sides to protect shoppers from the elements.

A 1946 Harold Spitznagel design, the Sears building is as stark as the South Dakota prairie. The facade of red brick is broken by eight sets of upper-level windows separated by squares of marble. Squares of polished rainbow granite are used around and below the storefront windows at street level. Within the recessed doorway before the threshold is the store's name written in script and inlaid in terrazzo.

This early 1900s view of Seventh Street shows a growing city.

Three

BUILDING THE BUREAUCRACY

Usually, terrible things that are done with the excuse that progress requires them are not really progress at all, but just terrible things.

—Edward Abbey

As a response to their important status, government buildings were normally high-style structures built with the finest materials and lavishly appointed with elaborate detail. This category of structure includes, not only city, county, state, and Federal buildings, but also human services institutions such as orphanages, special schools, and jails. Until the 1930s, government buildings were financed at the local, county, and state levels. The Great Depression era saw the infusion of federal dollars into construction projects. Some were fully or partially funded by New Deal relief programs such as the Works Progress Administration. Downtown has been blessed with a wide variety of government buildings exhibiting an impressive array of architectural designs. From the very small and simple 1903 city hall, to the magnificent Beaux-Arts Pennington County Courthouse, this community has taken pride in providing public employees comfortable and attractive work settings.

As the seat of county government, Rapid City is home to the 1922 Pennington County Courthouse. This grand structure is the third in a series of courthouse construction projects, with the two earlier buildings, dating from the early 1880s, having succumbed to fires.

Known to locals as the post office building, the federal building also housed numerous other federal agencies. It is a stunning neoclassical revival, Beaux-Arts edifice from 1912.

The notable 1915 Chicago school-styled fire hall had its beginnings in humble, wooden, garage-like buildings, housing the equipment of three separate hose companies that responded to fire emergencies.

Municipal government also supported cultural pursuits. As one of 25 Carnegie libraries built in South Dakota, Rapid City's became a city department when the classical revival building was constructed in 1915, as it was maintained with public monies. It replaced the old, wooden Library Hall that sat on the same site. The City Auditorium was an immense, brick entertainment venue, built in 1929 in the Gothic Revival style. It was demolished in the early 1970s.

Rapid City's first city hall was built in 1903. This one-story brick and wood rectangular building also housed the fire and police departments. The structure has colonial revival influences, a hip roof with roof crest decorative brickwork at the cornice line and an ornate central portico supported by Corinthian-style columns. Two tall, narrow, masonry-arched windows flank the entryway. Brick pilasters at the corners frame the main facade.

In 1955, at a cost of $128,118, the city contracted with M. A. Garland Construction to build a new municipal office structure at 22 Main Street. Designed by Ewing and Forrette, this modern two-story building rises 31 feet eight inches from a concrete foundation. The clean horizontal lines, symmetrical elevations, and low-slung roofline are reminiscent of prairie style architecture. The walls are haydite block with red and yellow face brick.

Rapid City's early fire department consisted of three hose companies organized in 1881, and a hook and ladder company. Fire fighting equipment of the day was horse-drawn and housed in these frame, garage-like structures, as pictured above. The department became formally organized in 1907. In 1915, a fire hall was built on Main Street. The two-story firehouse (right), constructed of brick and Fall River sandstone, exemplifies the Chicago school style. At street level, the primary facade contains five bays with segmented arches over three windows, a double vehicle entrance, and a pedestrian door. The upper level contains three bays with definitive, Chicago school-style, tripartite windows. Decorative elements include various styles of brick patterning such as herringbone. Interior spaces included living quarters for firemen, offices, and equipment storage. At the time it was built, the fire hall was considered the most modern in the state.

This 1887 county jail was built of brick and sandstone in an eclectic combination of Victorian Gothic and Italianate. Hips and gables formed the roofline below which ran a brick dentil course. Romanesque arches appeared in the gable ends. Contrasting brick was utilized for belt courses and windows exhibiting elliptical, segmental, and round arches. Lower level and mid-belt plinths served as sills for most of the windows.

Rapid City is the site of this 1922 Beaux-Arts-style county courthouse. The three-story edifice is faced with blocks of limestone and terra-cotta trim. The main facade exhibits four sets of paired, fluted, ionic columns. Three huge, two-story windows appear between them. A frieze and a denticulated cornice wrap the building. The main entrance displays medallions and a cartouche. On the sides, fluted pilasters divide bays containing large windows.

This Beaux-Arts-style edifice housed federal agencies, including the United States Postal Service, federal court, and the weather bureau. Constructed in 1912–1913 of sandstone, granite, and concrete, the two-story building exhibits five bays containing one-and-a-half story arched windows, a decorative concrete belt course, and five small bays with paired casement windows. The federal supervising architect favored this and related styles so as to encourage easy recognition of federal buildings.

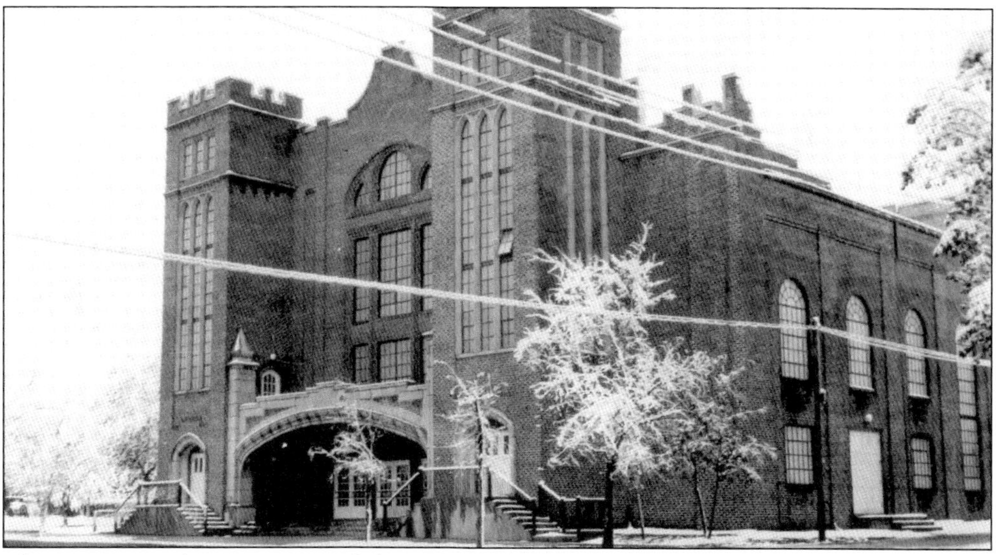

The 1920s saw the emergence of the civic auditorium as the popular venue for all types of events. This two-story, brick and stone edifice was one of the largest municipal auditoriums built in South Dakota in the 1920s. Designed by local architect James Ewing in 1929, it evoked the Gothic Revival style with tall lancet windows and crenellated towers on the front facade. This massive building cost $100,000 to construct.

Dedicated space for a library became a reality in 1881. Library Hall was a frame vernacular expression of the Italian Renaissance style. It exhibited symmetry, flat-arched windows, and a bracketed arched cornice. The building served as an opera house, cultural center, and entertainment venue until 1900. Between 1915 and 1917, a Carnegie library (below) was constructed under local architect H. E. Waldron, at a cost of $12,500. It is built of yellow limestone. The main facade is symmetrical, displaying two bays with three windows each on either side of a pedimented recessed central portico. Two pilasters and columns in antis distinguish the corners of the building. An entablature wraps the building, as does a low parapet. A 1938 Works Progress Administration project built carefully matched additions to each side of the building. It is one of 25 Carnegie libraries in South Dakota.

This is a 1919 advertisement for the services of Rapid City architect H. E. Waldron. He was responsible for numerous buildings throughout the city, such as the Carnegie library, the 1913 high school, the McNamara residence, and the Congregational church. He promotes himself as an architect and structural engineer, who has reasonable fees and provides efficient services. He claims, "to maintain one of the largest and best-equipped offices in the west."

The Alex Johnson Hotel has not yet been built in this mid-1920s photograph of St. Joseph Street.

Four

SAVING SOULS AND HEALING THE SICK

Remove not the ancient landmark, which thy fathers have set.

—Proverbs 22:28

Churches were among the earliest buildings constructed in frontier settlements. They served not only as spiritual and religious centers, but also as venues for social and cultural events. Missionaries from churches in the eastern Unites States were sent west, not only to establish churches among the Plains Indians, but to bring religion and civility to frontier mining and pioneer communities. These groups utilized private homes, rented halls, and schools until such time as monies could be raised to build suitable, dedicated spaces. Interdenominational churches were quickly established, incorporating differing religious groups who shared resources in order to maintain their spiritual lives.

The first churches were usually small wood vernacular structures with only minimal decoration, and perhaps a bell tower to distinguish them from other buildings. Design depended upon numerous factors besides the usual, such as finances and natural resources available. Worship practices, ethnicity, and denominational influences played a large part in what these houses of worship looked like. Later churches utilized pattern books and standardized building plans. But interpretations and subtle changes made by local builders provided distinctive custom-made structures. Larger congregations in more affluent areas were able to hire architects. The predominate style of early churches in Rapid City was some form of Gothic Revival. Other architectural styles represented were Romanesque, Renaissance Revival, and art deco.

Prior to the 1900s, hospitals had their beginnings in the homes of doctors with residences converted for that use. Historically, private groups created the institutions that cared for the infirmed. In Rapid City, formal hospitals began in private homes under the administration of Catholic and Protestant benevolent organizations. The nuns at St. John's Hospital and the lay Methodists at Methodist Deaconess Hospital presided over these health care facilities for over four decades. Expansions and additions were constructed as demand for services grew in concert with population growth. Architectural design accommodated advancing technologies and medical practices.

The first church organized in Rapid City was the Congregational Church in 1879. Their first church building was a small frame structure with Gothic styling, pictured above. It was built on a square plan with an apse in the front and a bell tower with a tall, slender steeple. The siding was painted green and the building came to be known as "the little green church." By 1914, the congregation had outgrown the little green church and hired architect H. E. Waldron to design their second house of worship. This two-story, rectangular, red brick building (below), costing $20,500, exemplifies the very formal Renaissance Revival style. It exhibits a projecting unembellished cornice, a parapet roofline, regular distribution of triple-hung hooded stained glass windows, and a pedimented gable over the central bay on the front facade. On the two flanking bays, each contains a raised pedimented main entrance.

The 1881 Immaculate Conception Catholic Church (above) was the first church built in Rapid City. At a cost of $345, it was a small front-gable frame building with Gothic-style features. The square bell tower formed the main entryway. Above the belfry, a tapered spire supported a Latin cross. The second Immaculate Conception Church (below) is the best example of Romanesque revival architecture in the city. Built of sandstone in 1909, it utilizes compound Romanesque arches for all openings. The top stones of the plinth wrapping the building serve as first floor windowsills. The crossed gables are topped by Latin cross finials. The front facade features a square 50-foot bell tower in which the main entrance is located. The tower exhibits four wide arched openings with balustrades. Fish scale shingles once covered the pyramidal steeple; they have since been replaced with terneplate.

The First Methodist Church was built on Kansas City Street in 1884–1885. Located at the site where the Masonic temple now stands, it cost $10,000 for both land and structure. The frame building (left) was carpenter Gothic with an ornate bell tower that accommodated the main entrance at its base. Decorative Victorian detailing was present in the gable verge boards, the bracketed dormered spire, and the pedimented portico. By 1919, the congregation had outgrown the wooden church and construction of a masonry edifice began. Completed in 1922, the new imposing brick building (below) with its crenellated bell tower, decorative brickwork, ocular windows, and concrete details is indicative of the late Gothic Revival style. In 1957, this church was destroyed by fire and replaced with the existing First Methodist Church built on the same location.

A stunning example of the English Gothic Revival architectural style, the Emmanuel Episcopal Church (above), built in 1887, exhibits rock-faced Lakota sandstone construction and lancet, stained glass windows. This style church usually features mass and structure over decoration, but Emmanuel church utilizes different shades of sandstone for trim, elaborate roof-cresting, and decorative shingles and timbering in the gable ends as decorative features. The church became a parish in 1891 and was debt-free by 1905. It was enlarged in the early 1940s, again in 1954, and again in 1991. In 1936, Pres. Franklin Roosevelt worshiped here. The interior exhibits open-timbered ceilings of dark-stained wood. This historic view of the chancel (below) also shows a shallow apse containing the altar, ambo, sedilia, and lantern lighting. Listed on the National Register of Historic Places, it is the oldest existing church in Rapid City.

The Presbyterians built their first church (left) in 1886. It was a frame vernacular structure, later used by the Christian Scientists. It was very plain with the exception of a bell tower reminiscent of the carpenter Gothic style. The second church (below) was constructed of large white sandstone blocks, reportedly quarried near Cowboy Hill. Completed in 1890, it was a cross-gable Gothic Revival structure with a decorative wood portico over the main entry. The elaborate yet graceful Roman-arched bell tower supported a pyramidal spire. The structure and tower exhibited decorative sandstone pilasters at the corners. All windows and other openings were round arches. Hardware and stained glass for windows were imported from Chicago. Decorative metal crests capped roof ridgelines. The neighboring manse was located north of the church. By the 1940s, the congregation had outgrown this building, which originally seated 300.

In 1951–1952, a new Presbyterian Church building was sited next to the old at 710 Kansas City Street. This new church is constructed of yellow and orange sandy dolomite from Minnesota. Trimwork and details are of concrete. The design is Gothic Revival, exhibiting cross-gables, lancet windows, and other pointed arch openings. Stained glass windows were eventually installed in 1961. The old church was demolished to erect an education building on the lot.

The 1941 art deco First Church of Christ Scientist building was designed by Christian Science architect Harry Edbrooke. The building is stucco and decorated with ornamental concrete slabs designed and made by Soren Neilson of Deadwood. It features the latest indoor fluorescent lighting of the time called night lighting. An unusual feature on the north side of the church is a combination sidewalk and gutter that carries away roof runoff.

The Bergen Lutheran Church was a Scandinavian Evangelical Lutheran congregation that built this Gothic Revival church on the corner of Eighth and Columbus Streets. A stone foundation supports a wooden structure with lancet windows and an entrance directly below the square bell tower with an oculus and pyramidal steeple. There is little decorative detail, yet a sublime elegance in its simplicity. This church was sold to the Baptists in 1890.

Built in 1909, the Swedish Free Church, affiliated with the Lutheran denomination, was a plain frame cross-gabled vernacular expression of the Gothic Revival style. It sits atop a sandstone foundation. It stands out as a house of worship only because of the lancet windows and the multi-paned paired lancet windows directly beneath the gable ends. The corner entry is unique and exhibits the pointed arch atop the double doors.

The Baptist congregation purchased its first church building (right) from the Scandinavian Evangelical Lutherans in 1890. The Baptists modified that simple structure with a small addition to the main entry, a sanctuary expansion, an oval versus round oculus, and decorative detailing such as verge boards in the expanded entry. When the school board purchased the church's land for expansion of the high school complex, the Baptists sold the church in 1912, and moved into a new brick building (below) on Kansas City Street. This neoclassical revival symmetrical edifice designed by H. E. Waldron exhibits three bays on the primary facade divided by paired pilasters. The central bay contains a pedimented entry with a Roman-arched window above it. A dentil row, a plain projecting cornice, and a pedimented parapet roofline wrap the building. Side elevations exhibit paired pilastered bays containing large tripartite pedimented windows.

Prominent South Dakota architect Harold Spitznagel designed the 1946 Trinity Lutheran Church, evoking a modernized Lutheran Church design with prairie style influences. Constructed of yellow brick, it features four square-sawed fossiliferous limestone columns, an 84-foot bell tower with a pyramidal spire, decorative geometric brickwork, and other religious, iconographic artistic details. The original building is 122 feet long and 46 feet wide, seating 680 persons. Spitznagel designed the parish house in 1953–1954.

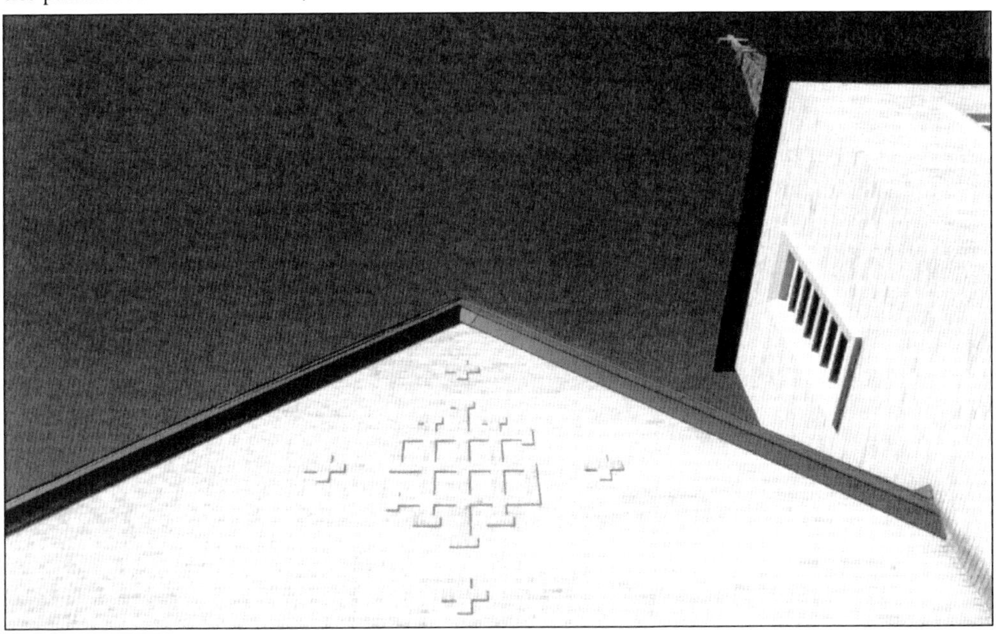

In brick relief, above the main entrance to Trinity Lutheran Church, is an IHS Christogram. A Latin adaptation for the Greek abbreviation of Jesus' name, *Iesus Hominibus Salvator* meaning Jesus, savior of mankind; it is also said to stand for "In His Service." Fifteenth century Franciscan disciple Bernadine of Sienna popularized IHS as a symbol of peace. Within this Christogram is a complex combination of Christian symbols.

One of the most influential architects in South Dakota was Harold Spitznagel, called "Spitz" by his friends. Spitznagel's architecture evolved over the years to a distinctly individual style reflecting the South Dakota landscape. Spitznagel believed the interior design was integral to the complete design and art was an essential element. Recognized for his contribution to South Dakota, Spitznagel was inducted into the South Dakota Hall of Fame in 2006.

Zion Lutheran congregation built this moderne-style influenced church in 1951, having outgrown the former Baptist church building they had occupied following its move to the corner of Fifth and Quincy Streets. Virtually void of ornamentation, but distinct in design, the stucco structure has rows of stacked windows, and brick trim around the entry, the side of the narthex, and along the foundation. The bell tower and cross emphasize the flat roof.

This classic Victorian Queen Anne home at Eighth and South Streets became the first Methodist Deaconess Hospital. It exhibits elaborate spindle work detailing such as the lace-like brackets, spandrels, turned porch supports and balusters, verge boards, and lacy brackets under overhangs left by cut-away bay windows. There is a second-story corner turreted porch and multi-bracketed projecting cornice. Roof cresting is visible on the hip roof with its multiple cross-gables and dormers.

In 1910, Dr. William Robinson started Rapid City's first hospital in his private home. A year later, the Methodist Church assumed management naming the facility the Methodist Deaconess Hospital. The Victorian house had 25 patient beds, a surgical suite, a "mother's room," an elevator, verandas, and a sun porch. New medical technologies required more space. Subsequent additions and expansions changed the appearance of the house to a more institutional look.

After a fire and several frame additions, Methodist Deaconess Hospital completed construction of its "fireproof" masonry addition in 1921. This brick and sandstone structure had a top layer of stone forming a plinth that served as the header for the first story windows. The top two stories were brick with a corbelled brick cornice and a brick parapet. Parts of the original frame house and subsequent additions were still visible.

The nurses's residence associated with Methodist Deaconess Hospital provided living quarters for nurses in close proximity to work. This Queen Anne–style frame house exhibited free classic sub-styling, displaying pedestaled classical columns in groupings of two and three. A steep hip roof with cross gables exhibited finials at the peaks. A bay window and an enclosed sleeping porch dominated the second story. Leaded windows were visible in the gable windows and others.

Another hospital began in a home west of downtown in 1926. Operated by Catholic Benedictine nuns, the Johnson House was welcomed by the community and expanded to five rented houses, becoming known as St. John's Hospital. A new brick and concrete structure, the center building pictured above, designed by J. H. Wheeler of St. Paul, Minnesota, was built in 1927. In the 1930s, two more structures, including a unique stone chapel (below), were added to the campus. The chapel's tile roof provided it with a mission-style feel. Its unusual round window's bottom halves pivoted to open. Services expanded in the 1940s necessitating additions to structures. In the early 1950s, a five-story wing was added on the southern-most building. Pilastered or projecting entry bays mark the main facade of each brick building, as does some minimal decoration and crosses. All the buildings are excellent examples of institutional architecture.

The Institute for Treatment and Care of Chronic Alcoholism and Drug Addiction, was located at Kansas City and Second Streets. Architecturally, the two-story home was a Queen Anne free classic, which was popular in the 1890s. It featured a hipped roof with lower cross-gables. Porch supports are classical columns on pedestals. Balusters are plain and closely spaced. Leaded windows appear in the gables, whose surfaces display decorative pattern shingles.

The Dawley Clinic, built in 1938, is a Harold Spitznagel design. The building, exhibiting prairie style influences, is constructed of brick with an asymmetrical entrance featuring black marble wrapping around to the front on one side while cross-shaped openings pierce a brick wall on the other. Black marble flows across the top of a brick planter incorporated into the primary facade as well as across the roofline.

This late 1890s view is of St. Joseph Street looking west from Fifth Street.

Five

Hallowed Halls

Whatever is goode in its kind ought to be preserv'd in respect for antiquity, as well as our present advantage, for the destruction can be profitable to none but such as live by it.

—Nicholas Hawksmoore, on the rebuilding of All Souls College, Oxford, 1715

In the process of town building, schools were a priority. They stood as tangible reminders of the value placed by a community on education. Like other early buildings, schools started as simple structures, sometimes made of sod or logs. As population demands increased, they evolved into larger frame and, eventually, masonry structures. Public schooling became available in 1878. Classes were held in rented quarters until 1881 when a building, constructed specifically as a school, was completed. In 1882, a stylish French Second Empire brick edifice was built to serve primary and secondary students. "Ward schools" moved primary students out of the Second Empire structure that then became Rapid City's first high school. As population grew, elementary schools were constructed, expanding out from the town center.

In 1913, a new building was constructed in front of the old and called New High School. In 1927, Pres. Calvin Coolidge utilized it as his summer White House. From Room 42, Coolidge announced his famous, "I do not choose to run for president in 1928." The building was forever after known as the Coolidge building.

A 1917 fire completely destroyed the 1882 building and damaged the Coolidge building. Washington Elementary School was constructed in 1918 on that same property. A subsequent building, Main High School was completed in 1937 east of the Coolidge building. A 1970 fire destroyed the elementary school and damaged the Coolidge building making it unsafe. Both were demolished. Main High School eventually became Dakota Middle School.

By the Territorial Legislative Act in 1885, the South Dakota School of Mines was located in Rapid City east of town. On the west side, federal dollars helped establish the Rapid City Indian School. Religious education became available when a Catholic school opened in 1917. At one time, Rapid City Business College was located in the Lewis Building at Eighth and St. Joseph Streets.

Rapid City's first masonry school building was constructed in 1882. This three-story, French Second Empire edifice had a mansard roof containing pedimented dormers with ornamental window surrounds. A rectangular bell tower took the school's height to 103 feet. Brick exterior walls displayed corbelling and quoining on the corners. Decorative brackets supported overhanging eaves. Displaying strong symmetry, a projecting central bay contained the main entrance flanked by tall four-over-four double-hung hooded windows.

In 1913, a new high school was constructed adjacent to the 1882 structure. This three-story brick, stone, and concrete building, called New High School and later, Coolidge, reflects the Beaux-Arts classical style. The main elevation contains seven bays; four recessed and three projecting. Two projecting bays contain pedimented main entrances at grade. The projecting central bay is pedimented at the parapet roofline. Brick corbelling supports a projecting cornice line.

Built in phases, Main High School was completed in 1937 and was connected to the Coolidge building. Reminiscent of Beaux-Arts classical design, it was four stories of brick, concrete, and plaster with a parapet roofline above a projecting cornice. The central bay on the primary facade contained the main entrance at grade. Double-hung windows were six-over-one. Floors were wood over cement while halls, stairways, and entrances were terrazzo.

This style, commonly utilized in schoolhouse architecture, has been dubbed collegiate Gothic. This was Immaculate Conception Catholic School, built in 1917. The two-and-one-half story, ten-room, square brick structure had a stepped and crenellated parapet roofline with concrete coping, below which ran a simple molded cornice line. Symmetrical bays flanked a projecting bay containing a double door entryway. Groupings of three windows, each with brick eyebrows, created a regular fenestration.

Lincoln School was built in 1908 at Ninth and St. Joseph Streets. This brick and limestone building was a vernacular expression of the Richardsonian Romanesque style, exhibiting strict symmetry and heavy, sturdy, masonry construction. A tripartite window appears over a Roman-arched main entry set in a protruding central bay. Other windows are 12-over-1 and double hung. It was sold to the city about 1950 for use as city hall.

Thomas Jefferson Elementary School was built in 1930. Constructed of brick and concrete in the Collegiate Gothic style, it exhibits a projecting central bay on the primary facade containing the main entrance between two brick, crenellated pilasters. Two flanking bays on each side of the entry bay exhibit strong symmetry in the placement of large casement windows and pilasters. Side facades are similar. Concrete coping caps the parapet roofline.

Built in 1918, Washington Elementary School was located on the high school campus behind the Coolidge High School building almost directly over the site of the first high school that had burned in 1917. This brick, one-story structure exhibiting classical revival elements had a centrally situated clerestory located on the flat roof. The building served in various educational capacities until it burned down in December 1970.

Rapid City Business College, built in 1919, alternately known as the Lewis building, was constructed of tan concrete brick in a simplified art deco style. This three-story institutional structure is at 802 St. Joseph Street. A concrete plinth divides the first from the upper stories. A wide cornice and decorative brickwork on the main facade exhibit simple art deco detailing. A storefront extension with a mission-style parapet was a later addition.

The National Humane Alliance fountain once stood in the intersection of Seventh and Main Streets.

Six

Dollars and Design

There may have been a time when preservation may have been about saving an old building here and there, but those days are gone. Preservation is in the business of saving communities and the values they embody.

—Richard Moe, president, National Trust for Historic Preservation

Late 19th-century banks in newly-formed frontier towns were small wooden false-front buildings so indistinguishable from other commercial structures that they usually appeared with a large sign indicating "Bank." From the late 1880s through the 1920s, when economies were enjoying more prosperous times, bank structures became more substantial and more architecturally discernible in an effort to convey a sense of security, stability, permanence, and prosperity. Thus, builders turned to the use of brick, stone, and concrete and embellished the buildings with the architectural detailing of the period. Corner entrances were very popular. Designs heavy with symmetry surrounding a central, pedimented entry led to the use of classical elements and detailing. Neoclassical revival, Romanesque, Renaissance Revival, and eclectic forms incorporating elements of all of the styles above also appeared in bank architecture. These amazing edifices became landmarks in most downtowns. Between the 1920s and 1940, very few banks were built in South Dakota, especially during the Great Depression.

As an architectural form, banks later moved into the modern era taking on the prevailing styles of the time for such institutional structures. Such styles included the moderne and international forms which made extensive use of steel, concrete, and glass.

Rapid City has seen an abundance of banking institutions rise and decline in the downtown core. The architecture has reflected the predominate styles of the period in which each was built as generally described above. Fire claimed one of the early bank buildings located on the southwest corner of Main and Sixth Streets. The eclectic sandstone was quickly rebuilt in the classical style. Rapid City National Bank reused the former Pennington State Bank building in 1934, until it moved to a new location and designed an art moderne structure. Since that time, banks have all been contemporary in design.

The first Pennington County Bank (above) was one of the largest banking establishments in Dakota Territory when built in 1888. Ornate and eclectic, it was built of brick and local sandstone, exhibiting Victorian-era Italianate and Romanesque detailing in the form of elaborate pediments and cornices, and heavy arched window surrounds. It had a conical turret above the corner entryway. This building burned in 1914. A new bank was built in 1915 on the same corner. This second Pennington County Bank (below) was a substantial two-story neoclassical revival granite and sandstone edifice. A massive decorative cornice wraps the north and east sides. An ornate parapet conceals a flat roof. On the east side, seven bays contain large plate glass windows with transoms on both levels, while the north, or primary facade, contains three bays with the elaborate entrance occupying the middle bay.

The First National Bank of Rapid City (above) was constructed in 1886. It was a two-story brick edifice with an ample multi-bracketed cornice, below which ran a decorative brick dentil course. Pilasters separated bays containing Roman and square-arched windows. A corner entry faced Main and Seventh Streets. Due to deterioration, the old building was torn down in 1913. In 1914, a new one (below) constructed of concrete and steel in the neoclassical revival style was built in its place. Two large fluted Ionic columns flank the main entry. The west elevation is divided into ten bays. The second floor contains seven tripartite double-hung windows. The first floor contains six similar windows with transoms. A western elevation addition added another entrance and storefront. The lobby is bronze, marble, and mahogany. A 1935 bank merger formed the First National Bank of the Black Hills.

The two-story Security Savings Bank (left), built in 1905, was located on the west side of Seventh Street next door to the Swander Grocery. Constructed of simulated cut stone blocks of cast concrete, it exhibits Romanesque Revival styling in the use of heavy Roman-arched window surrounds. Fanlights appear in the arched portion over the double-hung windows on both the first and second stories. A cast decorated cornice tops the structure. In 1928, Security Savings Bank moved around the corner into this utilitarian commercial building (below) on St. Joseph Street. The two-story brick building has art deco ornamentation. Partially obscured by snow from the blizzard of 1949, the south facade has four bays of equal size, two on each side of a central entryway, each of which house a canopied storefront divided by decorative brick pilasters. On the east, three large bays house one business's storefront.

Rapid City National Bank displayed art moderne styling. This 1942 yellow brick and concrete building exhibited cubic massing and streamlined horizontal elements. Walls were curved rather than square. When windows met at corners, minimal framing gave the illusion that the windows wrapped around the curve. Stacking rectangular lights in a sash created a new window style, accommodating the horizontally. The very vertical entryway contrasts with the rest of the building.

Built in 1959 at St. Joseph and Ninth Streets, the First National Bank featured a modern design of concrete, glass, metal, and stone. Concrete pilasters divided a smoked-glass curtain wall on the second level separated into grids of 12 panes each. At street level, some walls exhibited monolithic random mosaic veneers of red flagstone. Others contained floor-to-ceiling windows. A flagstone planter was nestled into a recessed corner entrance.

The federal building dominates the Southeast corner of St. Joseph and Eighth Streets.

Seven

Form Following Function

We may live without her (architecture), and worship without her, but we cannot remember without her.

—John Ruskin, *The Seven Lamps of Architecture*, 1849

The abundance of natural resources in the Black Hills created and sustained many business ventures that provided the basic necessities for town building. Mining, the initial reason people came to the region, continued to flourish beyond the glitter of precious metals. Materials for use in construction became a valuable resource. Thus, geologically-based industries such as the many quarries producing limestone, sandstone, and granite were able to thrive during the building of Rapid City and surrounding communities. Black Hills timber and lumber built the city's earliest structures until a building boom in the mid-1880s demanded brick. The right geology again contributed to the development of the numerous brickyards as well as the state-owned cement plant, and other businesses such as the Dakota Plaster Company.

During the 19th century, grain milling was the most important agriculture-related industry in the state. Mills and grain storage buildings such as elevators added to the built environment and downtown Rapid City has been home to several mills.

Food processing facilities such as creameries, breweries, and bakeries that provided staple goods established themselves along with their associated and unique buildings. In the late 1800s, Rapid City boasted factories with the capability to manufacture products including brick, brooms, cigars, lumber, furniture, and machine parts.

Public utilities such as telephone, electricity, and gas, each with long histories of their own and architectural forms specific to their functions, developed in order to provide the flourishing community with the latest most modern conveniences of the time.

Not all these types of buildings were necessarily architecturally significant, or even particularly attractive, and, in fact, many were built only with the thought to perform a specific function. Yet they all contributed to the building of a community by providing for the needs of the citizenry and therefore have a place in history.

Rapid City Gas Company was a manufacturing plant for production of gas from coal via the process of destructive distillation of bituminous coal producing gas for domestic and municipal purposes. The brick building featured tall, narrow, arched, multi-light windows housed in bays divided by brick pilasters. The rooflines were surmounted by monitor roofs with vents or small windows for ventilation. A multi-light ocular window appears in the front gable.

The first telephone arrived in town in 1881. Northwestern Bell Telephone Company built this two-story structure in 1929. The building was a vernacular combination of several architectural styles, including Gothic Revival and Italianate. It had reinforced concrete framing and floors, brick walls, stone and concrete trim, a tile roof, heavily bracketed eaves, and Roman-arched windows in the cross-gable ends. It housed business offices, the switchboard, and quarters for operators.

The Dakota Power Building on Main Street is a three-story, utilitarian-style structure that is part of the L-shaped Haines Block, wrapping around the corner bank building. It was constructed about 1918 of brown distinctive brick. It features strips of white stone accentuated by electric lights, a molded stone cornice, and a crenellated parapet. Copper-framed large plate-glass display windows flank a central recessed entryway. Architect H. E. Waldron designed this unique building.

In 1928, the Black Hills Power and Light transformer station was constructed on Canal Street in the area immediately west of the downtown known as the Gap. This is a utilitarian style building of brick and concrete with large multi-light industrial-type windows that allowed for adequate light and ventilation. Decoration is minimal consisting mainly of rows of brick corbelling and the crenellated parapet with concrete coping.

Black Hills Utilities Company occupied the ground floor of this 1918, two-story building on St. Joseph Street. This load bearing brick utilitarian-style structure has fixed-pane display windows and prismatic glass transoms on the storefront. The main entry is deeply recessed. Brick and concrete columns supporting the second story mark the storefront's corners. Paired double-hung wood windows with concrete sills appear between mid-belt concrete cornices. Concrete coping caps the parapet roofline.

Montana Dakota Utilities, formerly Black Hills Utilities Company, constructed this modern building on Kansas City Street in 1956. This two-story vernacular expression of the international style utilizes glass, metal, brick, and stone. The building exhibits a simple cubic "extruded rectangle" form. Large pane windows compose broken horizontal rows forming a grid creating facades where all angles are 90 degrees. Baseboard walls are faced with polished slabs of coarse-grained fractured gabbro.

The Schleuning brothers built the two-story Italianate commercial structure (above) on the left as a wholesale liquor store in 1897. In 1907, they built another Italianate immediately to the south, which was almost identical to its sister building. It was one of the last of this style built downtown. Both exhibit decorative bracketed metal cornices supported by pilasters serving to divide three bays in the upper level, each containing a narrow, arched window with brick window hood. Decorative mid-belt cornices appear above the storefronts each containing a recessed double-door entrance and large display windows. The upstairs once accommodated a boarding house, while the storefronts served numerous businesses including the Homecraft Bakery. This interior (below), photographed during the bakery's early occupation, displays a typical long narrow space with high ceilings. Clearly evident is a pressed tin ceiling and molding, a mezzanine level, and dropped lighting.

Jones and Company Bakery and Grocery was located at 613 Main Street. This is one of the ornate Italianate buildings housing huge fixed-pane display window storefronts with large prismatic glass transoms enclosed within embellished cast iron framing. Unusual signage spanning the width of the storefront is readable approaching from both directions. At this time, about 1907, downtown was unquestionably urban. Architectural styles, in both masonry and frame construction, shared the streetscape.

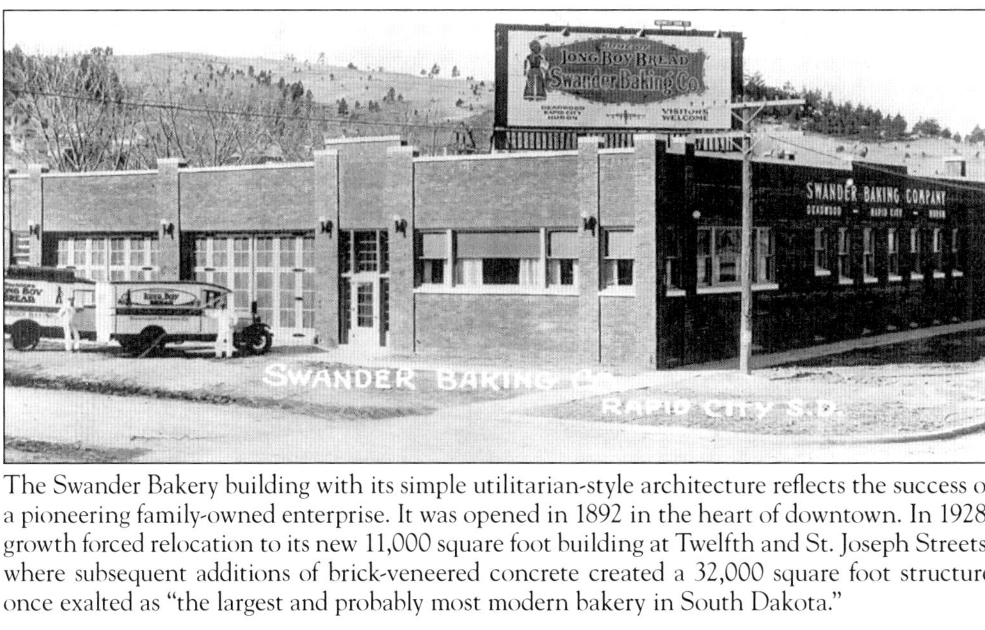

The Swander Bakery building with its simple utilitarian-style architecture reflects the success of a pioneering family-owned enterprise. It was opened in 1892 in the heart of downtown. In 1928, growth forced relocation to its new 11,000 square foot building at Twelfth and St. Joseph Streets, where subsequent additions of brick-veneered concrete created a 32,000 square foot structure once exalted as "the largest and probably most modern bakery in South Dakota."

Fred Finke arrived in Rapid City in 1886, opening up a cigar manufacturing and sales business. His shop was in the 600 block on the north side of St. Joseph Street in a false-front Italianate storefront. Ornate wood trim embellished the main entrance, the mid-belt cornice, the pilasters around the nine-light display windows, and the upper level window surrounds, adding a bit of elegance to an otherwise plain wooden building.

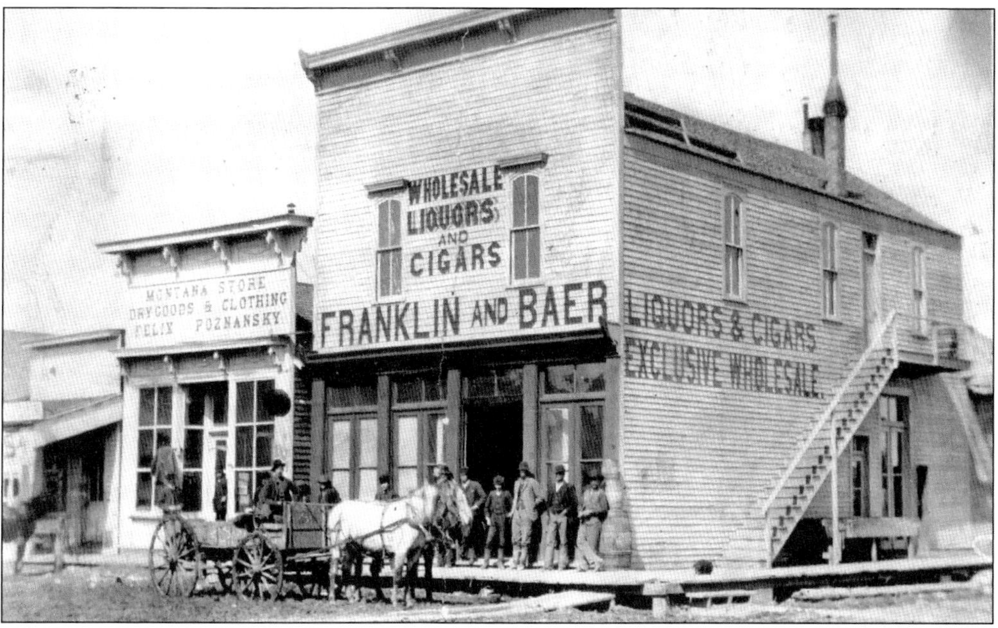

Franklin and Baer was a pioneer business and the largest supplier of wholesale liquors and cigars in early Rapid City. Housed in this two-story frame vernacular expression of an Italianate-style commercial building, the tall, false front gable-end structure was built on a rectangular plan. Located at the northwest corner of Main and Sixth Streets, this and two neighboring businesses relocated when the masonry Clower building was constructed in 1886.

Mills are more than buildings; they are large machines with architecture being fundamental to their function. The Gate City Roller Mill, built in 1883, was the most modern water-powered milling operation in the hills, producing fine flour utilizing steel rollers instead of millstones. Operating until 1890, this three-and-a-half-story frame building with stone foundation mirrored the architecture of 19th century mills. Windows were placed where needed and omitted where grain and storage areas required protection.

The McMahon Company, founded in 1896, served the needs of the area's agricultural and farming community. Expanding to six buildings by the railroad tracks, a grain elevator was added in 1911. The T. E. Ibberson Company of Minneapolis built the elevator, which has a gable roof and corrugated metal siding. The first structure was a single-story brick flat-roofed building with a roofline dentil course and eyebrows over openings providing minimal decoration.

Rapid River Milling Company was established in 1889 utilizing modern milling methods. The corrugated metal-clad building (above) was timber framed, and constructed of stacked wood. Periodic, unfavorable river conditions forced the mill to be supplemented by electrical power when purchased by Tri-State Milling in 1929. The high quality of local wheat enabled production of the famous Swans Down flour. In 1938, the old mill closed and Tri-State Milling began producing its flour in their new facility (below), which was considered the most modern in the nation. A six-story structure, with the latest innovations and equipment, produced 600 barrels a day. Typical for an industrial structure of its day, it has large sections of glass block on each floor providing natural light with pivot windows for ventilation. Somewhat decorative are vertical rows of glass block and the fluted concrete roofline emphasizing the art deco–influenced design.

Rapid City prided itself on its ability to stay current with industrial technologies and promoted its foundries and machine shops. The Homer Charles Foundry was one of these. This small complex of gable-end wooden board-and-batten vertically sided buildings house the differing equipment needed in the machinery process. Chimneys and venting features appear on the roofs. A furnace smokestack and windmill rise above the facility in the background.

The Downy-Wright Manufacturing Company was located here in 1907. In this industrial structure, they produced all manner of machinery in their foundry. The many windows and high ceilings guaranteed adequate lighting and ventilation. They utilized hydroelectric power available on the western limits of town. The company floundered, eventually shut down and remained vacant until the Crouch Line Railroad rented the building for use as a backshop. It burned in 1914.

Rapid City Lumber and Machinery Company was established in the late-1800s. The primary structure was a two-story masonry building with a corner entrance. The main facade was rusticated sandstone block at street level. Heavy round arches appear above the main entryway and display window. A sandstone plinth forms the sills of upper level windows and a division where brick construction begins. It strongly suggested a vernacular form of Romanesque Revival.

In 1928, John Knecht purchased the Daniel's Lumber Company located on the corner of Eighth and Omaha Streets. The original company office was a small wooden structure with a simple Italianate-style false front. Atop its roof's ridgeline was a large sign indicating the company name and phone number. This family business served the community for 51 years before expanding into housing and land development to form Knecht Industries.

This two-story utilitarian-style building, once located in the 400 block of Main Street, features a simple decorative art deco–influenced cornice and parapet. It was built on a rectangular plan out of what appears to be rusticated concrete brick. The main facade exhibits symmetry in placement of the two-over-two double hung windows flanking a central entryway. A rough-hewn stone lintel sits atop a single glass door with sidelights and transom.

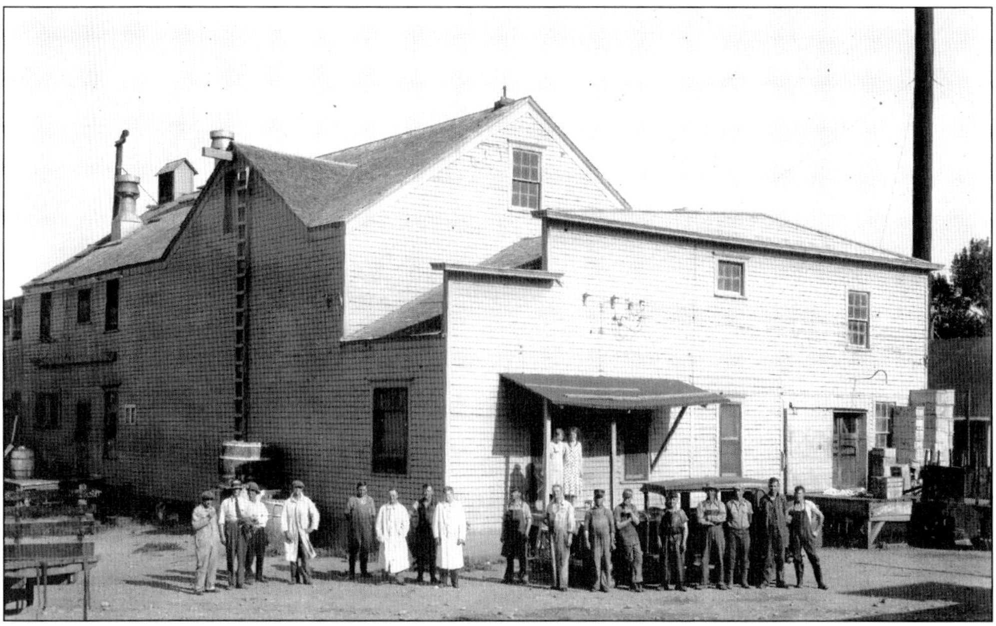

The production of dairy products was a profitable early industry in the region. In 1906, the second creamery in Rapid City, the North Star, was established and operated until it was sold in 1926 to the Fairmont Creamery Company of Nebraska. This building was a two-and-one-half story frame structure. As the company grew, this building was replaced with a new modern masonry structure with a cold storage plant.

Built in 1929, the two-story utilitarian industrial style Fairmont Creamery was designed by architect F. V. Thomas. Building materials were obtained locally: exterior brick was from Belle Fourche, while pink sandstone trim came from the noted Evans Quarry in Hot Springs. Despite its utilitarian nature, decorative brickwork, steel-framed multi-light factory windows, and a pedimented parapet roofline lend it character. For years, a memorable feature was an enormous milk bottle sitting atop the flat roof.

Inside the 1929 Fairmont Creamery, the interior walls are made of salt-glazed brick from St. Louis that is easy to keep clean with hot water or steam. Quarry tile floors were built on a slope to accommodate creamery processes. No dairy production has occurred on this site since 1971.

This scene at Sixth and Main Streets shows a thriving business district.

Eight

Elks, Masons, and Other Odd Fellows

When we build, let us think that we build forever.

—John Ruskin

Fraternal halls, lodges, and temples were very popular in South Dakota from the late 1890s to about 1915. Fraternal societies are associations of persons drawn together by common interests, experiences, occupations, or ethnicity and may be organized chiefly to provide companionship and pleasure for their members, as well as to furnish members with certain benefits or to help their communities. Such voluntary, nonprofit associations were established for the mutual aid and sociability of their members. These organizations are known for supporting charities and social work. Historically, membership was restricted and usually depended on invitations extended by members.

Throughout its history, Rapid City has had its share of such fraternal and social organizations including the Masons, Benevolent and Protective Order of Elks, Knights of Pythias, International Order of Odd Fellows, Knights of Columbus, Loyal Order of Moose, Kiwanis International, YMCA, etc. Most local groups utilized rented spaces. However, groups like the Elks followed the planning of many early fraternal buildings by constructing their facility to serve dual purposes; sharing lodge space on the upper floors with commercial activities on the street level. Others, like the Masons, known for erecting dedicated and sometimes elaborate structures, had their own building. Modest in comparison to their earlier, proposed structure, it is still a classic-style building in which the Masons take great pride.

Women's associations relative to the men's groups rose to recognition within the town. These included the Eastern Star and the Rebekahs. Other women's groups provided social, civic, and recreational support for the Rapid City's "fairer sex."

Rental spaces were available in quarters on the upper floors of commercial buildings as well as in Lewis' Hall. Mentioned frequently as a gathering place, it was also a billiards parlor, dance hall, and saloon on the main level. Most of Rapid City's early churches utilized the hall when they outgrew space provided in private homes.

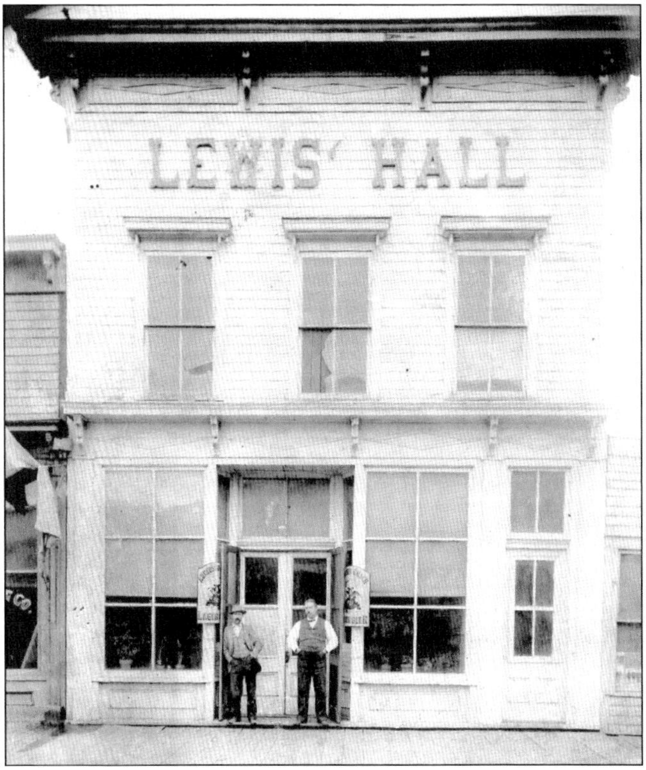

Before constructing their respective buildings, almost every early organization in town met at Lewis' Hall. Besides providing a meeting venue, this frame Italianate also housed a billiards parlor and dance hall. Above the two-over-two, double-hung upper story windows are simple bracketed window hoods. A diamond design decorates the bracketed cornice on the upper story as well as one above the storefront. Two, six-panel windows flank a double-door recessed entry.

J. P. Eisentraut designed the Elks Lodge in 1911, combining lavish club rooms and offices on upper floors with storefronts at street level. The yellow brick mission-style edifice displays concrete detailing. Classical influences are noted in the brown brick pilasters dividing the bays and the elaborate cornices. The foundation reportedly contains dinosaur footprints. Upper-story windows are Chicago-school style. The Elks Theatre was originally a lavish opera house that became an entertainment showplace.

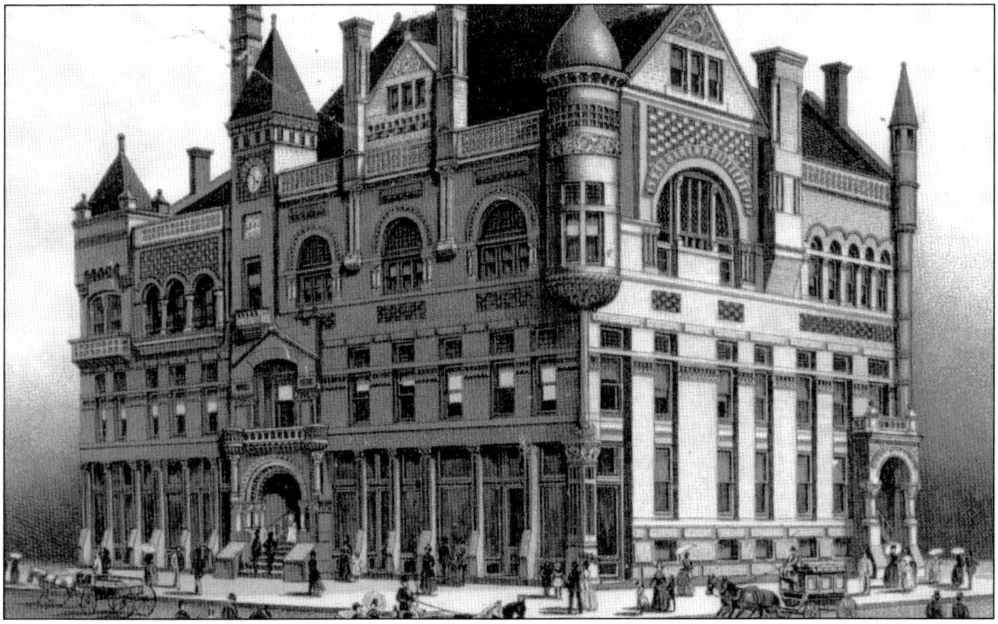

This is an architectural rendering of the lodge first proposed for the Rapid City Masons. Information accompanying this drawing indicated that it was planned for the northwest corner of Seventh and St. Joseph Streets. Construction got only as far as the excavation for the basement and foundation. "Hard times prevented completion." This would have been a wonderfully fanciful, eclectic structure. The Masons were known for building large and exotic temples.

The 1925 Masonic Lodge is an example of a simple neoclassical revival-style building. Located at 618 Kansas City Street, the tan brick edifice exhibits large Roman-arch multi-light windows, a pedimented entryway, two bays containing Ionic columns in antis flanking rectangular lattice windows, a decorative dentil row directly below the cornice line, and a plain parapet roofline. The rock surrounding the doorway is pale yellow fossiliferous dolomite from Minnesota.

This is a bird's-eye view of St. Joseph Street looking west to the Gap.

Nine

Rest and Recreation

When the past no longer illuminates the future, the spirit walks in darkness.

—de Tocqueville

Although life on the frontier did not allow much time for entertainment and recreation, pioneers sought out those opportunities and eventually constructed buildings and started businesses devoted to all manner of diversion and pastime. Ranging from legal and moral to illegal and immoral (as judged by the values and standards of the day), entertainment venues themselves ranged from elegant and formal to plain and vernacular. Since downtown was the focus of daily life, it was also the place to be for fun and fellowship. Downtown was the site of theatres and opera houses, museums, parks, bowling alleys, roller rinks, dance halls, auditoriums, saloons, pool halls, and gambling establishments. To some, even the "houses of prosperity" were considered an entertainment venue. Entertainment also took place on the streets with parades, circuses, tournaments, races, and competitions, drawing people to crowd sidewalks to revel in the fun.

Theaters and opera houses prospered. Traveling musicians, drama troupes, and local thespians entertained at Library Hall and Derthick's Auditorium before construction of the Elks Theatre. Much mention is made of the many saloons, but two stand out: Pete Sweeney's Bar and Big Jack Clower's Saloon. Known as cowboy headquarters, Big Jack's had a reputation for being the most dangerous and notorious of drinking establishments. The Alfalfa Palace was perhaps the most unique of all the local entertainment venues. Built in the heart of downtown, it was a wooden frame building covered with Alfalfa in decorative patterns. This was a festive marketing tool of the Alfalfa growers to promote local agricultural prosperity. It reflected a Midwestern and Plains tradition reminiscent of Europe's harvest festivals.

Downtown entertainment venues also supported and profited from the tourist trade when the automobile made the Black Hills a travel destination. Hotels, motels, and guest cottages played a major role in accommodating the influx of tourists. Beginning in 1927, visitors on their way to Mount Rushmore stopped here for diversions and necessities. Downtown saw many opportunities to capitalize on the burgeoning tourism industry.

The first hotel on Main Street was the Yankton House (above). Located on the south side of the street between Fifth and Sixth Streets, it was built in 1877 out of logs from the Black Hills. Grove Corwin and Dan Stafford built the structure, but the owners were from Yankton, Dakota Territory, which is how the hotel got the name. This rough-hewn plain building was two stories and had a hip roof. At this time, many of the structures, both commercial and residential, were of simple log construction. Following some interior and exterior improvements in 1878, the name was changed to the Merchants Exchange Hotel. Continued expansion and rehabilitation leads us to the accommodations pictured below in this 1887 photograph, exhibiting more stylistic features typical of the time, such as simple window hoods, decorative balusters on the balcony railing, double-hung windows, and a wooden shake-shingle roof.

The American House, one of the first hotels in town, was built in the late 1870s. It was a hip-roofed frame Victorian Italianate with decorative features especially noticeable on the second story porch balustrade, on the porch supports, and in the pedimented hoods over the windows and doors. The hotel, which served as the headquarters for the Sidney Black Hills Stage and Express Company, burned down between 1883 and 1884.

The International Hotel was another of the early hotels built in Rapid City. Constructed in 1878, the frame Italianate structure experienced numerous changes and expansions over time. The upper level porch balustrade exhibited simple Victorian ornamental millwork that also originally embellished the porch supports below. A paired, bracketed cornice supported overhanging eaves. The International was considered the finest hotel in the city until the Harney Hotel was built in 1886.

Simple and handsome, the Park Hotel on East Main Street reflected a vernacular expression of a Queen Anne domicile. Built in 1886 of brick and wood, it featured a wrap-around porch and a turret room. Porch supports were plain square posts. Tall narrow windows were paired and accented with contrasting brick eyebrows; second-story windows were similar. A tripartite window appears in the gable end. A plain bracketed cornice is visible.

The corner of Second and Main Streets was the location of the Reder Rooming House, the first such accommodation, built in 1887. This commodious building appears to have been built in two phases, one with a cross-gable roofline, and the other, a hip roof. The style may be considered Folk Victorian, exhibiting decorative millwork on porches and in gable ends. Also indicative are the elaborate window hoods and cornice brackets.

The Jester House (above) was a boarding house owned and operated by Lou Jester in the 1890s. Lacking any decorative detail, the house was a frame vernacular expression of the Queen Anne style with cross gables, tall narrow windows, and a wrap-around porch on the ground floor. In 1903, J. D. Patton bought and renovated the property into a reportedly quite good hotel. The Patton Hotel (below) sported a contrasting, two-tone paint scheme, and exhibited Italianate influences in the plain cornice with decorative brackets. By 1919, a café had been added and accommodations were advertised for $1 to $1.50 per day. Advertisements promoted a hotel policy, "If you have plenty you can stop at the Patton. If not, you can still stop if you are honest." It also boasted, "Pleasant surroundings, with flowers and lawn in summer."

The 1886 Harney Hotel was located at Main and Seventh Streets. This ornate Italianate style three-story hotel was brick with the main facade boasting a large cast iron and plate glass storefront. Striking features included the large, elaborately decorated and multi-bracketed cornice, the parapet roofline punctuated with finials, and the fancy pediments. Cast iron porticos marked the entrances. Until 1927, the Harney was considered the finest hotel in Dakota Territory.

In August 1927, at Sixth and St. Joseph Streets, ground was broken for what became downtown's most notable landmark. The Alex Johnson Hotel was commissioned by Chicago and Northwestern Railroad vice-president Alex Carlton Johnson. Designed by Edward Oldefest, it is Tudor Revival style with modern skyscraper form, evidenced in the half-timbered Alpine cap with gable end dormers. The remainder is fine red brick with terra-cotta quoining and detailing contributing decorative uniqueness.

Alex Johnson's respect for Lakota Sioux culture is visible in details of the hotel's interior design such as finish work, art, lighting fixtures, and furnishings created by Carlos de Lopez (above). Traditional colors, patterns, and symbols appear consistently throughout the building. Outside, above the street-level storefronts are terra-cotta Indian-head medallions (below), portraying profiles of warriors in feathered hair decoration. Natural elements appear in the immense fireplace, built with rounded Black Hills Precambrian quartzite boulders. The blending of the Plains Indian cultural heritage, classic Germanic, Tudor, and other European architecture, and art deco design motifs created a popular decor in western hotels during this period. At its opening in July 1928, the Alex Johnson Hotel was South Dakota's largest hotel, built to capture much of the 1920s tourism boom. It fulfilled Johnson's dream of building the "showplace of the West."

Rapid City's reputation as the "Gateway to the Black Hills" expanded with the advent of the automobile. Tourism began to supplant other industries as the leading commercial enterprise. Hotels flourished as did smaller tourist lodgings such as cabins, cottages, tourist courts, and motor hotels. An example of such a venture were the Arneson cottages. Frame and log exteriors provided the rustic feel expected by vacationers along with advertised "modern conveniences."

As a tourism destination and vacation venue, Rapid City hosted a variety of temporary accommodations. The Rushmore Motel, located on the eastern edge of downtown, took on a decidedly southwestern appearance. The mission-style roof parapet and the barrel-tile porch roofs, not to mention the stucco walls, and heavy headers and sill members on casement windows, provided a touch of the exotic among the usual more rustic accommodations of the region.

With 17 modern units opened year round, Harrington's Modern Court provided travelers roadside accommodations at 1215 St. Joseph Street. Motor courts flourished as automobile travel increased on expanded and improved roads and highways in the 1940s and 1950s. While many roadside lodgings relied upon gimmicks to attract tourists, Harrington's Modern Court relied on simple, frame, side and front gable cabins with air conditioning, a neatly maintained appearance, and adequate parking.

The Tip-Top Motor Hotel on St. Joseph Street was a shining example of the "civilized evolution" from tent to motel. Motor hotels appeared as single buildings of connected rooms in the shape of an *L*, *I*, or *U*, featuring an exterior corridor providing easy access to guest rooms and adjacent parking. Amenities included swimming pools, restaurants, coffee shops, bars, meeting rooms, lobbies, and in-room telephones. By 1960, there were 61,000 nationwide.

Derthick's, a commodious structure with a false-front, was built in the 1890s for roller-skating. Not successful, it was converted to stable use. Doc Derthick refurbished it, named it the Eureka and opened it again in 1907. A stage and large seating capacity gave it use as an opera house and theater. This venue remained until the Elks opera house opened. In 1913, it became an armory. It burned in 1927.

In the late 1880s, a practice unique to the Great Plains was the construction of grain palaces. In the tradition of European harvest festivals celebrating agricultural bounty, these structures were about attracting visitors and demonstrating abundance. The first Alfalfa Palace Exposition and Fair was held in 1917. Located in the heart of downtown, the palace was a square three-tiered building topped by a large four-sided dome completely covered in Alfalfa.

The Dreamland Theatre, located at 609 Main Street, opened for business in 1909. It was the fifth theater in Rapid City but the first billed exclusively as a "picture playhouse." It seated 380 persons. Housed in an Italianate-style brick building, it had a very ornate entrance that was brightly painted and adorned with angels and marquee style lighting. The ticket booth outside the main entrance was equipped with a megaphone to broadcast music.

Rapid Theater, originally the Rex, stood near the corner of Fifth and St. Joseph Streets. Built in 1928, it was updated with a metal panel curtain wall. Its name appears in art deco typestyle on vertical signage. A marquee sign advertises the current movie offering. The ticket booth is set to one side opposite large plate glass windows allowing a view into the lobby. A lighted canopy spans the front.

Rows of arched, two-over-two, double hung windows surround the upper story of the Round Up Bar and Rainbow Café with carved brackets seeming to hold up a projecting cornice. This frame vernacular Italianate influenced structure has an additional bracketed cornice dividing the traditional recessed storefronts from the "rooms for rent" above with transom windows evident on the Bar side. Neon signs advertise their services.

If there is one thing Rapid City had plenty of downtown, it was saloons. This particular establishment, with the somewhat whimsical name, was built in 1906 at 508 Main Street. The simple Italianate commercial building has a brick and rusticated sandstone block facade. Two display windows housed in a wood storefront flank the central, recessed entryway. A decorative cornice rises above a flat roof on this rectangular single-story building.

The Sioux Indian Museum (above) was a Works Progress Administration Project completed in 1938. Its style is rustic vernacular, designed by Waldo J. W. Winter (right), a National Park Service architect. The popular Adirondack rustic and craftsman styles of that period influenced the design. The overhanging eaves exhibit exposed rafter ends, ridge pieces, and purlins, all indicative of rustic styles. It is constructed of large Minnekahta limestone blocks. The foundation and chimneys are stone. Original fenestration included 23 tall narrow rectangular windows, two round windows, and a multi-light picture window. In 1957, a west wing was added to the rectangular building, making a T-shaped footprint. The addition, designed by local architect James Ewing, is compatible with the original design. Salvaged limestone blocks from the demolition of Lincoln Elementary School following its tenure as city hall, provided materials for the addition.

The trolley tracks are heading west down Main Street.

Ten

EPILOGUE

We will not be judged by the monuments we build but by those we have destroyed.

—Editorial, *New York Times*, October 30, 1963

The built environment frequently suffers at the hand of man and from the unpredictably of nature. Urban renewal, the highly controversial function of urban planning, reached its peak between the 1940s and the 1970s, resulting in large sections of cities' historic downtowns being destroyed to make way for highways and luxury housing. Many now consider it a failure.

Today in our communities, we are recognizing the advantages of historic preservation. Restoration creates an economic competitive edge and increases the appeal of the community.

While we are saddened by what we have lost, we are grateful for what has been preserved. Let us remain conscious of the fact that once a historical asset has been lost it cannot be replaced. Our cultural heritage reminds us of where we were and who we are. It should be considered a social and economic necessity.

This is the Harney Hotel as it looked in the early 1900s.

The Italianate ornamentation of the Harney Hotel had disappeared by the 1950s.

The Harney Hotel facade had changed dramatically by the 1960s.

The Harney Hotel was demolished in 1973.

The Municipal Auditorium was demolished in the early 1970s.

The south side of the 500 block of St. Joseph Street was demolished in the 1980s.

Tip-Top Motel, a 1954 classic, was demolished in 2004.

The 1912 Dakota Power Electric Plant was demolished in 2006.

GLOSSARY

Adirondack rustic	Style using native materials with rustic details.
art deco	Streamline design, geometric ornamentation and verticality.
apse	Alcove space behind the altar.
balustrade	A series of balusters with a rail.
barge board	A board, often ornately carved, fixed to the projected edge of a gable roof.
bay	Part of a building marked off by vertical elements, such as columns or pilasters.
Beaux-Arts	Classical style form: symmetrical, richly ornamented and of grand scale.
Carpenter Gothic	Gothic elements with scrolled ornamentation and lacy trim.
cartouche	An ornamental panel forming a scroll, circle or oval, often bearing an inscription.
Chicago style	Utilitarian design utilizing a steel frame skeleton for multistory buildings.
Collegiate Gothic	Gothic elements with brick exteriors and crenellated parapets.
corbel	Projecting brackets supporting a cornice, arch or oriel.
cornice	A horizontal molded projection crowning a building or wall.
craftsman	Style of low, broad proportions lacking ornamentation.
crenellated	Castle-like turrets or battlements.
cupola	A dome topping a roof or turret.
dentils	Molding consisting of small rectangular blocks resembling teeth.
distyle	Having two columns.
eastlake	Style emphasizing geometric shapes and simple elegant motifs.
edifice	Building of imposing appearance or size.
elliptical	An elongated circle.
entablature	Architectural elements supported by a column.
facade	A building's exterior face.
fenestration	Design and placement of windows in a building.
fossiliferous	Containing fossils.
gable roof	A pitched roof having a gable at each end.
gneiss	Rock composed of bands differing in color and composition.
Gothic	Style emphasizing pointed-arched features, fine wood and stone work and ornamental gables.
haydite	Expanded, vitrified shale.
herring bone	Pattern consisting of adjoining vertical rows of slanting lines.

hip roof	A roof with four sloping sides.
ionic	One of three classical styles of columns.
keystone	Central stone in the curve of an arch.
lintel	A supporting beam across the top of an opening.
mission	Style characteristic of early California Spanish missions.
moderne	Streamlined look with horizontal orientation.
neoclassical	Style based on the use of Roman and Greek forms.
oculus	A small circular window.
oriel	A bay window projecting from an upper floor.
parapet	A low retaining wall at a roof's edge.
pediment	Architectural element found on the front of buildings and above doors and windows.
pilaster	Shallow column projecting from a wall.
plinth	Projecting course of stones at the base of a wall.
portico	Roofed entrance porch supported by columns.
prairie style	Low, horizontal style with emphasis on natural materials.
purlins	Horizontal timbers supporting roof rafters.
Queen Anne	Decoratively rich Victorian style.
quoin	Stone or brick used to accentuate a building's corners.
Romanesque	Resembling ancient Roman architecture.
Second Empire	French influenced style featuring mansard roofs and tower elements.
terminus	The end of something; final point.
terneplate	Lead and tin alloy used for plating.
transom	Glass pane above a door or window.
tripartite	Composed of three parts.
Tudor	Style characteristic of medieval buildings.
utilitarian	Style emphasizing utility and function.
vernacular	Architecture indigenous to a specific place.
Victorian	Stylistic period of architecture, 1860s to 1900.